Independently published in paperba
JV Publishing
Tel: 07726366424
jvpublishing@yahoo.com

ISBN-13: 9798354917709

Dedication

This is dedicated to all my family, both near and far, and to those no longer here – especially my mum and dad, who made me the person I am.

Acknowledgements

Firstly, to my friends in the U3A, who I have gathered with each month since 2018, for our meetings and to tell our stories. Thank you for the great times we have. All this would not have been possible without Louise who started this group and has kept me going over the years. Her inspiration and help, along with the wonderful subject ideas, have been a constant help.

Thanks also to Vicky and John Regan from JV Publishing for their invaluable help in completing this task.

I'd like to thank my family for allowing me to go public with some of these tales from our past. I hope they enjoy reading these memories that we share.

Finally, to my long-suffering husband and partner, Vic, who has encouraged me to do this, despite a lot of our togetherness time now being shared by others.

I hope you enjoy reading these stories and that they bring back similar memories from your own past.

To every thing there is a season (1611)
Anonymous

This verse is from the book of Ecclesiastes, in The King James version of the Bible.

To every thing there is a season, and a time to every purpose under the heaven:
A time to be born, and a time to die; a time to plant, and a time to pluck up that which is planted;
A time to kill, and a time to heal; a time to break down, and a time to build up;
A time to weep, and a time to laugh; a time to mourn, and a time to dance;
A time to cast away stones, and a time to gather stones together; a time to embrace, and a time to refrain from embracing;
A time to get, and a time to lose; a time to keep, and a time to cast away;
A time to rend, and a time to sew; a time to keep silence, and a time to speak;
A time to love, and a time to hate; a time of war, and a time of peace.

Stories from a Jar
A Life Remembered

By
Vicki Makins

Chapter One

A Picture Worth a Thousand Words

This memory for my book concerns my late mother, Evelyn Joyce Russell, nee Wallace. She was always known as Joyce.

In 2013, we received the sad news that my favourite Aunt Kitty had died. She was one of my mum's five sisters and the closest in friendship with my mum. She had no children, so the task fell to two of my other aunts, her sisters-in-law, to sort out and clear the house of all her things as they lived the nearest to her home in Romford, Essex.

As I knew that Aunt Kit had a great friendship with Mum, I asked my Auntie Beryl – who was mainly doing the sorting – to look for Mum's World War II medal and any photographs that would have been suitable for me and my family. My mum was in the army for nine years prior to and during the war. This was before I was born.

After a few months passed, I had a phone call from Aunt Beryl to say that they had not found her medal but had come across an album of photographs that Mum had put together during her time in the army and would I like it?

Firstly, this came as a great surprise as while I had seen some photos of my mum's army days, this was the first I knew of this album. In my mum's words to myself and my sisters, 'I did have a life before I had you lot.'

Aunt Beryl posted the album to me. By this time, I had moved to Saltburn and was now living in the north. Imagine the surprises this album revealed. Full of photographs of my mum's life in the army and with friends and colleagues she had.

She was in the army for nine years from 1939 when she joined at the start of the war aged seventeen. She was an *Ack-Ack* girl in the ATS, as it was then known. This means she worked on and manned the guns, including firing them at enemy planes.

She did tell us about this aspect of her life but never really talked much about where she had been posted to, apart from in Norfolk,

291 (M)H.A.A. BATTERY, ROYAL ARTILLERY.

GRANGETOWN. MAY 1948.

where we used to live. Therefore, I could not get over it when I came across the attached photograph in the album.

As you will see, it is a group shot of her regiment taken in Grangetown in May 1948. She is in the second row from the front – the fifth one in from the right.

At first, I thought this was the Grangetown near here, then noticed that it was taken in Sunderland. I have since researched this online and discovered there was an army camp during the war near Grangetown in Sunderland. So, that is where she was in the latter part of her time in the army. She was an officer by then, a Warrant

Officer Class II.

What a small world it is. This photo shows how strange it is that I have moved to the north and now live not too far from where she spent a good part of her life before becoming my mother.

Chapter Two

Memories of Christmas

As I have gotten older, and more significantly in recent years, I have realised that the build-up, the work, the anticipation, and of course, the excitement that comes with the arrival of Christmas is often heaps better than the actual event itself,

So, I have thought back to when this build-up was especially true for me. This is particularly significant as today is what is still celebrated in Germany, and other parts of the continent, as St Nicholas Day, December 6th.

In the early 1970s, two of my sisters and I were at a boarding school in a place called Hamm, which is near Munster in Germany – then the west. It was Windsor Girls' school, and nearby it was Windsor Boys' school a little further up the road. These were service secondary schools for the forces' children – RAF and Army – stationed in Germany at the time. There was no secondary school on the camp my dad was posted to, so we had to go here. We were there for three years and used to come home in the holidays on the trains, and parents were able to visit in the quarter terms.

It was a school run by the British Families Educational Service and all the teachers were English, but the rest of the staff there were German, which I will write about further in the book. The school was divided into seven houses. They were split between the various accommodation blocks on the site, the main school building, the

9

dining hall, a gym, a sick bay, and our own chapel and church.

My sisters and I were placed in Edinburgh House, and our matron Frau Schroder was particularly strict.

Thinking back now, I understand why because being a sort of mum to a couple of hundred girls per house aged from eleven to nineteen was no easy task. We ranged from good and bad at various times in the school year.

In keeping with the German traditions, our Christmas at school began on the evening of December 6th, *St Nicholas' Nacht*. This is traditionally the start of present giving, initiated by St Nicholas, or Santa Claus.

The matrons encouraged us to put our cleaned shoes outside our dormitory doors in the evening before bedtime. If we had been good, we found a treat of wrapped sweets in the shoes the next morning, but if naughty, we were given small twigs. So, for my first two years at Windsor, I am sorry to admit I had twigs in mine.

However, I had grown up a bit by my third year there when I was nearly seventeen. More privileges came as I was given further responsibilities as a House Prefect.

One of these was to be the Head of table in the dining room. There were six pupils at a table, and the annual treat before the end of the Christmas term was to decorate the tables for Christmas with various decorations of the season for our last evening supper together before going home for the holidays. A prize was given for the best table.

In my last year there, the task fell to me to collect a little pocket money from everyone on the table for our Christmas decoration funds. Then the biggest treat was when we were allowed at the weekend into Hamm, the town, on the local buses to shop for Christmas table goodies and gifts for the season. The buses are long bendy ones, and the local population certainly knew when the girls from the school were allowed out. There was a sea of red berets on the bus and much chattering and excitement. The younger pupils had to go out with matron, of course, as a chaperone.

It was wonderful to see Hamm all lit up with the lights in the town and in the big stores. We also loved when the whole school would go to the Paluskirche (cathedral) in Hamm for the annual carol service. It was magical – all lit up for Christmas and the sound of singing. We had all been practising our hymns and carols for weeks in school.

All the girls were dressed in their best uniforms, representing our country in Germany so, we were on our best behaviour.

The last night before we went home for Christmas, we gathered around the large Christmas tree decorated by us all at the end of our house corridors and sang carols. I particularly remember singing *Stille Nacht* in German at this time.

Then there was the hustle and bustle and excitement of us all heading to the station in Hamm to get the trains home to our much-missed families. The sight of the streaming toilet rolls on the trees just outside our school as we left was a reminder that we were all going home for Christmas at last.

Chapter Three

A Bookshelf Revisited

Coming from a services background as I do – my dad joined the RAF when I was two – I never had the opportunity to live near or see much of my relatives. They were in Essex, and we lived too far to see them or visit often. In addition, cars and roads were not as efficient in the early 1960s as they are now.

My grandma, my dad's mother, lived in Dagenham, at 78 St George's Road. It was a council house in a part of the Greater London expansion area from the East End after the Second World War. The East End had been heavily bombed, and that is where a lot of my family came from.

My grandfather, whom I never really knew, had been in the Merchant Navy and was away an awful lot. Going to Grandma's house was an experience. It was filled with items and souvenirs he had brought home from his many trips to sea. I remember carved men from Japan and a fire screen in the front room where Grandma used to do her sewing on an old Singer treadle machine in front of the window. There were lots of interesting objects in her home.

However, in those days, television did not wind up and start until the early evening, and being young and full of life, the days at Grandma's house were long. Apart from listening to the grown-up's conversation and playing as quietly as we could, boredom often set in. Grandma, whilst a wonderful lady, was a product of Victorian values and upbringing and told us many times that in her day, children should be seen and not heard. A sentiment that perhaps today could be revised now and again, I think.

Our lovely dad took my sisters and me to the library while Grandma and Mum got the dinner ready to assuage boredom and get us out of the way for a while. I think this was in Barking and not too far away. So, we caught the tube from the station close to Grandma's house, and, as I was about seven or eight and my sisters about five, this was, of course, quite an adventure.

I remember the library was an ancient Victorian building that looked quite dirty from the outside. But, of course, everyone had coal fires in those days, and buildings were dark and drab.

My dad loved books, and it follows that we have all got the love of them and reading from him. Going into the library that first time was a wonderful experience. I had never seen as many books.

The first shelf I came to in the children's section had a range of books with titles like Tales of the Ancient Greeks, Myths and Legends. Also, Tales of the Romans and their Myths, Tales of the Norsemen, Ancient China and others from places like Persia and Egypt.

On opening the first books, I was engrossed in the contents and sometimes by the wonderful illustrations. So, I became hooked for life on these ancient tales and began my lifelong love of history and language.

When I found one about the Tales of King Arthur in Ancient Britain, this began a lifelong love of this period with the Tales of the Knights of the Round table.

Later, when I was married and with my own daughters, we would go for holidays to Somerset to find Glastonbury and see the Castle of Tintagel and the places in these stories from my imagination.

After that first visit to that library, I took a few books out to cover our stay whilst visiting Grandma and read them avidly. The days passed so quickly that I knew what I would be reading the next time we visited.

13

As a final thought, it is strange that I have come across other people who share my interest in these ancient tales, like the actor Stephen Fry who I was at college with in later years. He happened to be on the radio only a couple of weeks ago talking about his love of these tales and his recent book *Mythos: The Greek Myths retold.* It seems I am not the only person interested in this era when growing up. It is another example of the *Small World* we all live in.

Chapter Four

A Matter of Life and/or Death

It is said that a cat has nine lives. So, I have concluded that if I was a cat, I would have already lost three of mine because I had three events in my youth that could have resulted in my demise. The first experience occurred in the summer of 1967 when I was almost twelve. We lived in Norfolk in a rural area, about nine miles from the picturesque town of Wells-next-the-Sea. We often went there at the weekends as a family and spent many times at the beach. Sometimes we used to go *cockling* as Wells is famous for the so-called *Stiffkey Blues*.

It is a beautiful and popular place with a large sandy beach when the tide is out. However, there is a channel of water before the sea, on the sand, which forms when the tide starts to come in, then the main beach in front of that.

Subsequently, when the tide starts to come in, it happens quickly, and the channel fills up with a fast current. I now know this to my cost.

When we were there that summer, I spent some time with my family but was pleased to see my friend and her family sitting near us. We decided to go off, by ourselves, for a walk along the beach. We crossed the shallow, only ankle-deep and made our way to the sandy stretch just before the open sea. It was quite a narrow channel then, and we sat on the sand for a long time, talking and dreaming as young girls do. Finally, after a good couple of hours, we decided it was time to return and join our families. We walked towards the channel of water, but by that time, it had filled up and gotten wider and, as we soon found out, was much deeper. We thought it would be easier to get across, but we were wrong. The currents had come, and we were soon out of our depths. The water was now up to our waists and rising quickly. It was a terrifying moment. Our parents on the other side of the channel waved at us frantically and told us to go back, but we couldn't. The water was getting deeper and higher and was almost up to my neck. I was scared. This continued until the next thing I knew, a boat came towards us. It was the coast guard sent to rescue us. I shall never forget the relief when the men pulled us into the boat, and we were returned to our waiting families. The feeling of nearly being drowned stayed with me for a long time after that day.

The second incident happened to me the following year, in July 1968. I have attached the newspaper cuttings from my scrapbook at the time.

We lived in a rural area on an RAF camp in north Norfolk. There were only two buses a week to the nearest towns of King's Lynn and Fakenham, and it was common for – especially younger people – to hitchhike to get to Fakenham, which was nearer if you couldn't get a lift. There weren't as many cars then.

My friend and I got the bus into Fakenham on the day in question but missed the only bus home and decided to walk. It was about eight miles. Unfortunately, I was knocked over on the side of the road by a hit-and-run driver, although they were caught later.

I have no memory of the accident to this day and ended up in the local hospital in King's Lynn, where I was in a coma for a few days. I was lucky to have survived. What a trial it must have been for my parents, particularly as my dad was abroad at the time on detachment. My mum must have been very strong, but I can say, although she was naturally concerned about me, I was still in trouble for walking back, even though I had been injured.

The whole situation ended up in court when the drivers of the car, two young men, were found guilty and fined.

Another lesson was learnt by me at that time too.

The third event occurred again in the summer. It was 1969 and was a couple of days before the end of the summer term at the two secondary schools attended by all the pupils in the catchment areas near Fakenham.

We had not been long on the school bus coming home when the driver unexpectedly turned up a side road known as *Dunton Patch*, not far from Fakenham.

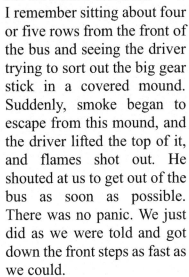

I remember sitting about four or five rows from the front of the bus and seeing the driver trying to sort out the big gear stick in a covered mound. Suddenly, smoke began to escape from this mound, and the driver lifted the top of it, and flames shot out. He shouted at us to get out of the bus as soon as possible. There was no panic. We just did as we were told and got down the front steps as fast as we could.

I remember standing outside the bus on the grass verge, watching the children towards the back of the bus. They were banging at the emergency exit window located at the rear and trying frantically to get it open. Flames were rushing up the bus, and it was terrifying.

Eventually, the emergency exit window opened, and the children at the back poured out onto the grass and pavement below. I only found out afterwards that no one was hurt apart from one girl with cuts. We were all fortunate that the bus driver was quick thinking too. He got out of the front windscreen of the bus, which he had

17

smashed. The bus was completely wrecked, and we had to wait for relief buses to take us home. Once again, I was lucky but dread to think what it must have been like for my poor parents, wondering where I was, late home from school that day. There were no mobile phones in those days. The enclosed newspaper cutting shows a picture of the completely burnt-out bus and further details.

All in all, a fortunate situation for me and the others. I am lucky I'm still here after all these frightening events.

Chapter Five

A Tearful Reunion

The year 2000, the start of the new millennium, was a special year for us and the beginning of the new century.

It was our silver wedding anniversary, twenty-five years, and although we had celebrated in other ways, like having a holiday, we decided it would be nice to have a party too. Parties are a tradition in my family.

We made a list of family and friends we would like to invite, and colleagues from our workplaces too. Invitations were sent to America and Okinawa, where my sisters lived. However, I did not expect them to come all this way to see us as they had all been over only three years before for the sad and sudden loss of our dad. All three of my sisters married into the American services, and we do not see much of each other. The loss of both our parents within four years was a trying and traumatic time for us all. They all came over to help with the funeral arrangements and sort Dad's house and possessions, but it was such a difficult time when we had to say goodbye and go our separate ways.

So, when my husband, Vic, and I decided to have our party, it was a big surprise to hear they would all be able to come and help us celebrate. It would be nice to be all together for a happy occasion this time.

Our anniversary is in March, but we thought a summer celebration would be better, so we planned the party for August. We booked a hotel in Norwich so that other family members could stay over if they wanted to and not have to travel back home that night. However, I wanted my three sisters to stay at our house. This was great for me, but I don't know if Vic was as pleased as we planned to have our two daughters back from university. It was too expensive for my sisters' husbands and families to come over, so Vic was the only male in the house in the days leading up to the party. As he said, he had to take tickets for the bathroom! We had some fun and laughs during those days.

The most tearful reunion at this time was when we went to Norwich Airport to meet Lee. Lee and Debra are identical twins, and our youngest sister is Kerry. Debra and Kerry arrived from the US via Heathrow and then caught the train to Norwich a few days earlier. It was such a special moment when we all went together to welcome the last of our sisters. Lee flew from Okinawa and had to change planes three times, ending her journey at Norwich Airport.

Vic drove us to the airport, and we all stood in the café, looking out the window, waiting for her plane to come in. This final part of her journey was coming from Schipol, Amsterdam. We craned our necks to watch for her coming down the plane steps, and when we spotted her, we all waved and cried out. There were tears then but even more when she came through the arrivals area. As you would expect, we were hugging, and it was very emotional.

We returned to our house for more hugs from our daughters, who had not seen their aunties since Dad's funeral.

We had our party with all our family and friends, and it was wonderful. We had a memorable time going out with my sisters while they stayed with us but sadly, the time came for them to leave, and we parted again. The four of us haven't been together since that time, which is a by-product of service life, but those memories of our reunion are special.

Chapter Six

A Room in a Home

In our early married life in 1977, we moved into our first house. It was in a Victorian terrace of houses in Woburn Street, which is close to the city centre of Norwich. They were built in approximately 1864 as the date is engraved on the end of the terrace.

The rest of the area near Woburn Street was bombed during the Second World War, but these houses withstood it and remained. Finally, after years of neglect and being left empty, the city council decided to pull the terrace down. This was in the early 1970s.

Thankfully, the Broadland Housing Authority Housing Association stepped in for us as new tenants and compulsorily purchased them. Furthermore, they decided on a renovation programme for each house, which was duly completed. This modernisation becomes relevant later as I explain about *our room*.

We lived there from 1977 and brought up our family of two daughters. We had many happy times as we watched them grow. After a few years, I returned to working part-time. While our girls were settled into the local Middle School, we came across *our room*. The house was in the middle of a terrace row, which meant you entered via the front door into a long hallway. Before you stepped into the kitchen, there was a large hall cupboard at the other end. We had filled this with all the usual junk like our Hoover, cleaning brushes etc., and Vic had put hooks on the side wall to hang up our outside coats so they were out of sight.

One day, sometime in the early part of 1984, we decided to investigate a strange musty smell which seemed to be coming from the hall cupboard for some time. Our curiosity had become aroused. Vic had several conversations with neighbours who thought there may have been a basement to the house, as there were some in similar situations in other parts of Norwich. This was possible with the houses having been there for over one hundred years.

After a while, he decided to look and started pulling up a couple of wooden floorboards covering the floor of the hall cupboard. As more space was made, he could see what looked like a lot of rubble, which looked strange, and he said he would investigate further. Putting on his overalls, Vic pulled up another floorboard until there was enough room for him to go down and get onto the rubble.

I was watching and nagging him to be careful as I saw him disappear. Finally, after a few moments, he said, 'You're not going to believe this, but there is a room down here.' Of course, I was amazed as well as shocked.

A while later, Vic managed to come back up into the hallway, and said it looked like the cellar of the house, but it was now full of rubble, and impossible to see much.

We had a discussion and concluded that when the house was renovated in the early 1970s, the builders simply dumped all the rubble and bricks no longer needed down this cellar and closed it up.

This presented us with the possibility that we could use the old cellar by turning it into another room. Having a growing family, there was always scope for more space.

However, the main problem was getting rid of all the rubbish and debris before we could do this. Sometime later, Vic and his brother went back into the cellar over two weekends to get out all the rubbish and old bricks. They brought it all up by hand to the ground level in buckets. We hired a couple of skips for the time, and they were filled to capacity.

When some of the mountainous pile of debris had been removed, I went to look around the now discovered room. We were amazed to see there were still the remains of old servant bells on one wall, as well as the old coal chute on another. Also, on the ground was a great big piece of marble which we figured may have been the top of the old table down there. These were mainly used for pastry making and had just been left by the previous builders.

Despite it being a tough and dirty job to clear the cellar by hand, we were excited to plan what we could do next to turn it into a serviceable room. We took out a loan and hired builders and plasterers to renovate the room to make it usable. The walls and ceiling had to be rendered, a damp course put in, and a window to let in some light. Also, they put in a staircase from the cellar to the upstairs part, which was now part of our old hall cupboard, as it was quite a long way to get down once the rubble had been cleared. Vic did the electrics.

Once all this had been done, we decorated and eventually, the girls had their toys down there. Next, we put some basic furniture down, and it became their playroom. They spent many happy hours there and had their own space. In addition, the room became useful as an extra place for family to stay a couple of times when they visited.

This was in 1984, and we made great use of this room for a good few years after. However, as is usually the way, a few years later, we decided to move to an altogether bigger and better house in a different area. We moved in 1991 when the girls began their secondary education.

Adding the extra room helped put a little value on the house, which benefited us. It certainly added to our memories of our fourteen years living in that house.

Chapter Seven

Impact of a Favourite Toy

At Christmas, when I was about seven, I got a present from my paternal grandmother, which probably became the start of a lifetime's collection and subsequent interest in dolls dressed in National Costume.

She had made me a doll dressed in a Spanish costume, complete with a mantilla (hair headdress). Grandma was clever with the needle and made this without a pattern.

She had a treadle sewing machine in the front room of her house in Dagenham. When we visited her, she was nearly always sitting there sewing or making something out of old bits and pieces. My love and interest in sewing comes from those days of watching her. Her father was a tailor, so it must be in the family.

The doll came to have pride of place on a table in my bedroom, and in the next few years, it began to have more dolls to stand with it. I received two more made in bridal costumes, which a great aunt, one of Grandma's sisters, had made and dressed for me. Then Grandma made me another one in a blue costume which looked like a nun. I loved the feel of the skirt's material as it was velvet and soft. I played with them for a while, but as my collection grew, it became a hobby.

In the early 1960s, you used to be able to buy collections of dolls in a box. I don't know if you still can today. I don't see them much in toy stores. Over the years, though, I received two of these collections as gifts. One set had six dolls dressed in the National Costume of countries such as Yugoslavia, France, Germany, Spain, Hungary and Japan. I found this particularly interesting when I was young as the dolls' costumes were all different and distinctive, with headdresses and patterned skirts. My fascination grew and gave me a further interest in finding out about these places with strange names that the dolls represented. This was added to when in those days, the annual Eurovision Song Contest often had singers and dancers representing their chosen country and in National dress. This is no longer the same.

This started my interest in places around the world. Of course, it was helped by the fact that as my dad was in the RAF, he used to go away a lot to work in different places abroad, sometimes when on a detachment. When he returned, he often brought gifts for my sisters and me, consisting of a doll from that country.

I particularly loved the little one he brought me back from Nice, in France when he was there. He brought another favourite of mine, from Germany. This one still has pride of place in my cabinet at the front. She is dressed in the costume of the Black Forest region and has a distinctive straw hat with big red pompoms.

There are a couple of musical dolls in the cabinet that I received as gifts. One is dressed in a costume from old Russia, and it plays *Lara's* theme from *Dr Zhivago*. As a child, I loved playing this.

Now to the Cabinet. As the years went by, my collection of dolls grew, and they were taking over my bedroom. Then, when my little sister, Kerry, was born and I was nearly nine, we moved again to Norfolk, and as we had three bedrooms, she eventually came to share with me. Of course, as she got older, I had to prevent her from touching my things, so it was not ideal.

After a while, Mum gave me the cabinet that had belonged to her mother, my Nannie, for my dolls. I was over the moon, and the dolls have lived there ever since.

Over the years, they have been put in there, and packed away into boxes when we moved, and come out again and returned to the cabinet in time. They have become well-travelled dolls for real.

As I became an adult, I gained a few more dolls for my collection. If I knew family and friends were going abroad, I would ask them to get me a doll from the country they visited. Also, I bought one or two myself, such as from Spain and some nice dolls dressed as Cowboys and Native Americans from the USA. I also have one from Mexico, which my mum brought me back.

Then when I got married, we moved in with my husband's nanna for the first six months, whilst we were looking for a flat in Norwich. Of course, there was not much room in our bedroom, but still, I had to bring the doll's cabinet as it was the only furniture I had. So, the cabinet has been with us in three houses in Norwich and now sits in our home in Saltburn. It is full now, and there is no room for more.

The dolls cabinet	The Doll that Grandma made me when I was about seven and started my collection.

27

The dolls in it are nearly as well travelled as the costumes they wear, representing their countries. When I look at them, I realise each has a story to tell of the places they represent in the world or the people they are connected with, now gone but still in my heart.

> **One of my favourite dolls, brought back from Nice by my dad in the early 1960s**

Chapter Eight

Menu from a Memorable day and Favourite Outfit

My fiftieth year was on 6th November 2005. After much talk and discussion with my family, we decided to celebrate the occasion in a special way. Some months before, and by mutual consent, we decided to go for a cream tea at the Ritz in London. Our eldest daughter, Stephanie and her partner, Andrew, made all the arrangements and booked it in advance, so it

was a complete change for me.

We subsequently found and booked a convenient Travel Lodge in the centre of London to stay, as we wanted to make a weekend of it. I bought myself an outfit for the occasion, made of a pretty pink and black material with flowers. This was sparkly and covered in gold sequins. It was a top and skirt to match, and I had matching shoes to wear with it. At the time, I thought it suited me, and I felt very glamorous in it, especially as my husband and daughters complimented me on it too. Of course, the girls and the men all had to dress smartly for the occasion as the Ritz has a strict dress code, and men had to wear a shirt and tie.

We drove to London early on the Saturday morning and booked into the hotel. The Ritz is in Piccadilly, near Green Park Underground station. The tea there was booked for approximately three in the afternoon.

On arrival there, I was taken aback by the splendour of the surroundings and the fabulous décor and lighting. There was a grand piano as you entered the foyer room. Later, it was played by a pianist, which added to the relaxing atmosphere. We were ushered into the dining room by a smartly dressed waiter in a red waistcoat and a velvet bow tie, and this was the beginning of us being waited on for the rest of the afternoon.

We were shown to the table, and I loved how the waiters pulled out our chairs for us to sit down. We were then given the menus. The tables in the room were laid with pure white cloths. The tableware was the finest bone china with pretty patterns of flowers, along with

real silver teapots and the silver tea service with dinky silver teaspoons. Very posh. The menu consisted of dainty sandwiches of cucumber and cream cheese, cream cheese and tomato, smoked salmon, egg and cress, ham and tomato and more choices.

All the sandwiches had had their crusts cut off, of course. This was followed by small cakes of every shape and description. Cream horns, Victoria sandwich tarts, chocolate finger cakes and then cream scones with jam and fresh cream, all served separately in silver dishes with silver ladles and spoons. We tucked into these lovely treats with gusto, and it was nice to be together.

The tea was a choice of Ceylon tea, Darjeeling, Indian, Bergamot and more, including fruit teas and lemon and camomile tea. We had all these items brought to us by the smart waiters and could have as much as we wanted and more should we ask for it.

The sandwiches and cakes were brought in on a couple of beautiful cake stands of bone china with about four layers. All the tea was in the wonderful matching tea service. There were tea strainers on little cups as the tea was loose. No tea bags here.

Our afternoon passed most pleasantly, and it made for a wonderful

memory. Especially when a small cake was brought out for me to blow out the candle on, and everyone sang *Happy Birthday* to me, including the waiters.

After our lovely afternoon at the Ritz, we returned to the hotel for a little rest. Later, we went to the West End, as my family had bought tickets to see the musical, *We will Rock You* with the music of the group Queen, as a further treat. It was on at the Dominion Theatre.

It was fantastic, and although my feet were killing me by this time, the high heels I was still wearing did not prevent me from loving every minute of the day we had just had.

I shall never forget the lovely tea at the Ritz and consider myself lucky to have been there with my family.

31

Chapter Nine

A Trip Back to School

My memories of schooldays are perhaps not the same as many peoples', as I grew up with my dad in the RAF. This meant that I went to a few different schools in many places, though it is true to say I did not attend as many schools as some of my friends may have.

That is to say, I went to five primary schools from the age of five to eleven and just two Secondary schools. I had friends who had gone to at least a dozen of each, depending on where their fathers had been stationed.

Me, in Singapore.
Aged about five, standing near the banana tree in our garden

Primary Schools – My first school was at RAF Seletar in Singapore, which I started at age five. It was from approximately 1959-1962. As the weather and climate are hot there, being in the tropics of the Far East, school only took place in the mornings, and we went home at lunchtime to rest in the afternoons. So, my memories of this time are a little hazy, but I remember the heat. At least there are a lot of photos from our family's time in Singapore.

My next experience of school was when we returned to England in 1962. We had to live for over six months with my grandmothers in Essex, whilst my dad had to wait for a Quarter on the base where he was stationed for the next three years – that is what base housing is called in the Services.

We lived first with my nannie in Romford for a while, and I attended the local primary school in Rush Green, where she lived. I do remember my nannie taking me to school sometimes. I must have been about six, and I remember it was an old school, and the weather was much colder in England.

After a few months, we moved to live with my paternal grandmother in Dagenham. I think my nannie's house had become a bit more crowded as I had a lot of aunts and uncles who were all still living there then. So, I went to the local primary school at the end of Grandma's road.

My main memories of that time are trying to make friends with the other children. A Service child's young life is difficult as you know you may not be there at that school for long and saying goodbye to friends you have made becomes very hard. It is usually an emotional wrench, but it becomes something you learn to cope with. It also aids your independence, and children are resilient.

In late 1962, we eventually moved to RAF Odiham in Hampshire. I went to the RAF school on the base, and my memories of this are also hazy. I do remember playing with the other children, though, and I loved attending school. My old school reports show I did quite well in my lessons.

In 1964, my dad was posted to RAF West Raynham in Norfolk. He worked there on the Kestrel squadron, a joint enterprise set up with the German and USAF services in the early days of NATO. However, we as a family lived at RAF Sculthorpe, which was not far away. As we were a family of six by then, we required a three-bedroom house and were allocated a place just outside the camp, addressed as 6 WOQ. As we lived away from the camp, we had to

33

attend the catchment school in the local village called Syderstone. My sisters Lee and Debra were at school by then, and I had to take them with me every day in all weathers. It was nearly a two-mile walk to the school in the village and again at the end of the day. There were no buses, and as Mum didn't drive, there was no alternative.

There were only two classes at Syderstone VC primary school, one for the older children I was in and one for the younger ones my sisters were in. Our years there were, for all of us, full of memories, some good and some bad, but that is another story.

We were at this school for a number of years until I took the eleven plus exam and then later went to the grammar school in nearby Fakenham. My sisters then began to go to school on the camp after this.

Secondary Schools – In 1967, I went up to the grammar school in nearby Fakenham after passing the eleven plus on the second attempt.

I travelled in and back every day on the local school bus, which also held the pupils for the Secondary Modern school in Fakenham. This transport had lots of noise and rivalry between the two schools as I remember.

The grammar school was a great change to the school I had been used to in Syderstone, as it was much bigger and had lots more pupils, being the school which served a large catchment area of this part of North Norfolk. Also, the classrooms were many, and we had to change to different ones for most subjects. I now had a timetable as there were many new subjects to learn. Also, lots of different teachers too. I had a hockey stick and a games kit, all new to me then. My three years at the grammar school were a lot of fun and, on the whole, enjoyable, and I had some new friends too.

Then came the time when I had to leave. In 1970, Dad was posted to Germany for three years, just as I was about to take my options for my GCEs, as they were then. So, we moved to RAF Laarbruch, in what was then West Germany. We lived quite close to the Dutch border in RAF accommodation near a village called Weeze, about five miles outside the camp. However, there was no secondary school on the camp, so my sisters and I had to attend a Service boarding school in a town called Hamm. This was in the region of North Rhine Westphalia and was quite a distance away, as were many other schools at that time run by the BFES system

First day at Windsor Girls' School. September 1970

(British Forces Education Service). The school was Windsor Girls' School, and there was Windsor Boys' as well.

As it was a long way to travel, the school laid on trains to take us and bring us home for each beginning and end of term. The first day we went there on the train was an experience. There were students everywhere and luggage and personal items like guitars and sports equipment. It reminds me of a scene from a Harry Potter film, on the *Hogwarts* train. We were at Windsor for three years, and it was an experience you'd never forget. I was lucky to

The former houses of Windsor Girls' school

have my two sisters for company, but many were alone, and homesickness was great for some.

However, it taught us independence from an early age and helped in the growing up process. It was disciplined, and, although I did not recognise it at the time, it was necessary with so many adolescent girls there away from home. I took my O levels there and learnt a lot about life too.

Some years later, in 1996, my husband and I were on holiday in Germany visiting friends and one of my sisters who lived in

35

Bitburg. We decided to finish the holiday with a bit of a tour around some of the country. We managed to find Hamm at my request so I could return and re-visit my old school WGS.

However, things did not bode well when Vic asked me where the school was, and I said, 'I don't know.' The fact was that I had been a lot younger then and we went by train with school escorts and parents to look after us. There was a lot going on with the travelling, and we ignored directions to the schools. Finally, we stopped at a local polizei station in Hamm and asked for directions, but the police did not speak much English. However, they knew where the old schools were and kindly escorted us there, which was good of them. Our residence in Hamm at the schools for over thirty years had obviously left a mark on the town, not least because it gave employment too.

I believe the school buildings are still there but no longer used as schools, closing in the 1980s. They reverted to German military ownership and are now turned into refugee blocks, mainly for Eastern Europeans crossing the borders.

After getting permission to wander around, we went into the areas where the school's former buildings were. It was a real trip down memory lane for me. Outwardly everything all looked the same.

Chapter Ten

A Hidden Talent

I have a hidden talent that not many people apart from my family and, unless you know me well, are aware of – I can sew and make clothes, as in dressmaking.

This skill is probably inherited through my genes as in my family, my great grandfather, Joseph Dean (1859-1905), was a tailor by trade. This family, on my father's side, came from the old East End of London and lived in the area of Bethnal Green and Stepney. According to the 1881 census, Joseph Dean Snr was a tailor's cutter at twenty-one and worked in a clothing cutting room in Mile End Old town.

Detailed on the 1901 census is that he was married then to my great grandmother Maria, and they had seven children. His son, Joseph Dean Jnr (my great uncle), is named as a tailor's cutter. One of the daughters, my grandma Ellen (known as Nell), was an expert seamstress.

On the 1914 census, all the family lived on Old Ford Road in Mile End. It says it was above a haberdashery shop which I feel was entirely appropriate to their trade.

When we visited my grandmother Nell in Dagenham, where she lived, she often used to be at her Singer treadle sewing machine

37

facing the front room window. She was always mending or making something, often from old, recycled garments. She wore an overall, full of patches where she had repaired it. So, I have concluded that my skills and love of sewing come from her.

When I was about twelve, I started to develop an interest in the fashions of the day. This was in the 1960s when fashion and pop culture began, and I used to read magazines of the time, such as *Jackie* and *Biba*. The mini skirt was invented by Mary Quant, but as I knew my mum couldn't afford to buy the latest styles then, the only option was to make them yourself.

I had started grammar school by then and as doing needlework was one of my subjects, the skills I began learning there were put into practice. My first project at school was to make a DS (domestic science) apron. Although this was all right, it was hardly a fashion garment, so in my spare time at home, I began looking at making a few things for myself to wear. My mum had a sewing machine, and she let me use it and helped me with the patterns etc.

It came to be that I made many of my clothes then. I particularly remember going to the shops and the markets, mainly in Fakenham and King's Lynn, to look at the patterns and choose the materials. I loved the feel of the different types of cloth and still do.

I remember making myself a mini skirt in my early teens out of a particularly bright and colourful pattern with lots of swirls and shapes. This was known as *psychedelic* then, and it was mainly bright pink.

When I went to WGS in 1970 after moving to Germany, I had been doing needlework, which meant I was put straight into the subject to study at GCE or O level as it was then. Unfortunately, this meant I never got to wear my DS apron as I never learnt cookery and DS at school.

For my final exams in needlecraft and dress, I had to make an outfit and a piece of collage or tapestry. I chose to make a two-piece suit out of a dark blue velvet material which consisted of a midi skirt and a waistcoat, all lined inside. I made a blue, patterned blouse with a dog-eared collar to wear with the suit. These items were all the fashion then. I chose the material and accessories from a shop in Hamm when I went with the girls on our two-hour weekly outings on a Saturday afternoon.

I remember the struggle it was to make the fasteners on the waistcoat out of a cord piping material in the shape of frogs, as they were known.

The collage was a picture of houses on a tapestry in the old style of a typical German street. My mum later had this made into a picture in a frame which I still have. I wore the outfit I made too.

I am pleased to say I passed my O level in needlecraft and dress. The skills I learned, and the enjoyment I got in sewing helped me make my own clothes from then on.

When Vic and I decided to get married in 1975, money was short, and as I was still a student, I thought I would make my own wedding dress. Vic had bought me a sewing machine a little before this as he knew I loved sewing. Thus, it came in useful.

I made my dress, going to the shops in King's Lynn to choose the pattern and material. This was in between my college classes at the time.

After a few years, when our family came along, I used to make a lot of their clothes too. Having girls, it was probably easier to make little dresses for them than shorts for boys. I put the machine to good use by making curtains for our first two houses and other household items such as cushions, mats, aprons and a couple of bags for our outings to the beach.

I made the dresses for my girls when they were the flower girls at Kerry's wedding.

I still have the sewing machine, but my use of it has dropped off over the years. Clothes are cheaper to buy nowadays. It is not a saving to make your own, and I don't have the patience I used to have either. However, I still have the same pleasure I always had when I get the urge to make something myself. Which I occasionally do.

Chapter Eleven

A Brush with Celebrity

In 1973, I left Germany with my family as my dad's tour ended. He was posted back to Norfolk to the same base where we had lived. This was quite unusual, but I suppose it was to do with where the planes were sent to be based.

We moved back to RAF Sculthorpe, where we lived at 701A Coventry Street. I was seventeen and at a crossroads in my life, I feel, looking back now. I had left Windsor school in the middle of my A levels, and at a time when I was almost grown-up, it was harder than ever to leave friends and people I knew behind. So, I did not know what to do.

After much thought and decision-making, I concluded I did not want to return to school but did not feel ready to go to work full time either. So, it seemed the next best thing was to attend college instead and finish my A levels, even though it would mean starting again. I had enjoyed freedom and independence for quite a while, and the thought of returning to school and being forever in school uniform did not appeal.

I applied and was accepted to the nearest technical college in King's Lynn, some twenty miles away. This was known as the Norfolk College of Arts and Technology or NORCAT. It is now known as the College of West Anglia.

Due to the distance, I had to go by bus and stay in a hostel in the town with other students from Monday to Friday, coming home at the weekends. Again, I think this was arranged by the RAF, as there were few buses – only once a week – and we lived in a rural area.

My independence at boarding school helped a lot with this period, and I enjoyed my whole time at college. Finally, I was almost an adult, and at last, I could be one.

So, I studied English, History & RE at A level, and it was in my English and History lectures I first met Stephen.

He stood out from the start. Although most of the other students and I wore fashionable clothes of the 1970s – such as one friend who used to have tartan strips on the bottom of her jeans like the Bay City Rollers – Stephen often dressed in clothes reminiscent of the Edwardian era. As he told us, Oscar Wilde was his hero.

This was helped by studying two of Oscar Wilde's plays in English. From the start, the rest of the class and I became aware that Stephen was suited to the characters he played. He was *Ernest* to a tee. In the play, he became an excellent *King Lear*, and I read opposite him as *Cordelia.*

After a while of being there during our studies, one of my sisters, Lee, came to attend the college and became a member of the drama group outside lesson time. Shakespeare's play was subsequently produced – *A Midsummer Night's Dream.* Stephen naturally had a major part in this play, being *Oberon,* but my sister was in it as one of the fairies. So, my sister acted too, and the play was produced and put on for the public, and we went to see it in due course. It was a sign of things to come for Stephen.

When the time came to take our A level exams, it was a strange thing for us in the class that Stephen did not turn up, and despite thinking he would sail through, he was not there. It was years later we found out why.

I am, of course, talking about meeting Stephen Fry, who is now famous in literature and drama. He has been dubbed a *National Treasure* in the words of the media.

He has been honest and forthright about his battle with bipolar disorder, or manic depression as it used to be called. I now know

41

that this was the cause of his absence when we took our exams. In one of his autobiographies, he told years later about how he was in prison for taking a credit card, and this incident occurred at the time I am talking about. So, after this, he went on to finish his studies at Norwich Technical College and subsequently went to Cambridge. He became one of the founder members of the Cambridge Footlights brigade and has been famous and popular ever since. I have followed his career with interest.

Many years later, after I was married and we moved to Norwich, it was advertised that Stephen would be in the local bookstore to sign copies of his latest book. Of course, I had to go. The crowds were all around the block, and I joined them. I probably waited half an hour or so to be in the line to meet him and ask him to sign my copy of his book.

It was strange for me to start talking to him about our mutual time at King's Lynn college, but he said he did remember, and we chatted for a bit and then he signed my book. Vic was in the background and took this photo to show that I have had more than a brush with this celebrity.

Chapter Twelve

A Special Something

My special something comes out of the cupboard only at Christmas. It reminds me of Christmases past, when I was a little girl, and before I grew up and became a mother myself. It always evokes memories of a time before all the responsibilities of being an adult began. This is because it once belonged to my parents and has been passed down to me. It is a musical decanter for brandy to be put in.

My parents won it in a Whist Drive in Singapore in the early 1960s when we lived there. They had a wonderful life in Singapore, as it was for many Europeans based there after the Second World War. When not working in the RAF, Dad and Mum attended Whist Drives a lot, which were regularly held on

43

the camp. The photos I have show the good times they had. Although they had a young family, they knew the importance of time out for themselves and their interests.

When we returned to the UK in 1963, this object was always part of our lives. It used to stand on Mum's sideboard in all the houses we moved to when I was young. I was forever asking Mum to put it on so I could watch the dancers. I loved watching them move and jig to the music. I was fascinated – even more when people and family came to stay, especially at Christmas, when Mum used to fill it up with that bronze liquid, and you could still see the dancers performing through it.

I think my love of ballet and all things to do with dance came from that object.

I loved it so much that I used to say to Mum, 'When you die, can I have that?' Of course, I was young, and it was the innocence of childhood saying that. Little did I realise that one day it would be true.

We lost our parents relatively young at seventy and seventy-three, respectively. I was only thirty-six, and my sisters were thirty-four and twenty-eight – it was truly a terrible shock to become orphans at our young ages. So, to receive this object was a bitter-sweet gift.

However, as time wore on – and time is a healer, as the saying goes – the sight and sound of the dancers in the glass is a lovely memory of wonderful parents and childhood memories long ago.

Our parents may not be here now, but they are always with us, and when I bring out the object, especially at Christmas, it reminds me of happy times and special memories.

Chapter Thirteen

A Painful Memory

Today January 9th, is a part of my painful memory as it was my mother's birthday. She died in 1992, six months after her seventieth birthday. As time has passed, the pain has diminished, as it does, but it is always there. It is a double sadness for my family and me, as tomorrow, January 10th, is the anniversary of Dad passing away. The dates are linked as he had been to the crematorium to take flowers on Mum's birthday the day before.

When my dad retired from the RAF in 1976, they and my sisters moved to Bretton, a new development just outside Peterborough.

They had a lot of good years there, and we all had happy times as a family. Then in the early 1990s, Mum got progressively worse with her rheumatoid arthritis, so much so she couldn't get about very well or do things she loved to do with her hands. Dad became her carer and looked after her, but being a determined and independent woman, she hated being dependent on him and others. She went into hospital when she got pneumonia in the summer of 1992 and gave up the ghost rather than carry on as she was. This we believe was the case, and we were all broken-hearted, but none more so than our dad, who had lost his soul mate. I never saw my dad cry until he lost Mum. Then he never stopped.

We all had to be there for him, but it mainly fell on me, the eldest, as all my sisters were abroad at the time. We wanted him to move to Norwich, where we lived, but he wouldn't as he said his life was in Peterborough, which it was. It is only now I am in the same age bracket and position in life that my parents were then that I can understand it.

After four years of living on his own, he seemed to be coping, but we will never know, as on January 9th in 1997, he went to the crematorium as he often did, and I called him in the morning as I always did, and he didn't sound well at all. Maybe he caught a chill, but I think it was the whole experience of the day. It was the last time I spoke to him.

When the 10th came, it was a Saturday, and I rang him in the morning, but there was no answer. I thought perhaps he had gone out to get a paper and got on with my day. Having a teenage daughter and husband at home – our eldest daughter had just returned to York University after the holidays – and a full-time job myself, my life was always hectic. I tried calling Dad again later. Still no answer.

By the time the late afternoon came, my own life had taken over, and I didn't think about Dad until early evening when I called again. Still no answer. I tried again within the hour, and still silence. I thought at first, he may have gone to bed as he wasn't feeling well but still couldn't fight the feeling that something was wrong.

We settled down in the evening to watch the telly, but my mind was constantly on Dad. No mobiles then, of course, and no answer from the phone, and no one else to call. He was alone in Peterborough apart from the neighbours, who didn't appear to be there either, so I had to call the police. We were watching Casualty on the TV when I called, and I have never seen it since, as it always reminds me of that time. I explained to the Norwich Police who I was, where Dad was, how he wasn't answering my calls and asked whether they would investigate with their people in Bretton. Vic and I were, of course, worried sick, and I had begun pacing by then but couldn't help it.

Then came the knock on the door, within an hour of calling them.

I knew who it was. Two policemen came in and told us the worst news.

Their colleagues had had to break the door down of Dad's house to go in, and there they found him, alone and on his bed. They said it had probably been a heart attack, and this is what the doctor put on his death certificate later.

However, the rest of my family and I know he truly died of a broken heart – missing our mum so much. They had a good marriage.

After the police left, we were, of course, in shock. The police told me he had been taken away because he had died alone. As I was his next of kin, I had to go to Peterborough to the hospital and identify him the next day. The shock and pain were unbearable and still are even now. The thought of him being alone at the end was the worst, but now, after all these years, I feel that perhaps it being quick is the best way to go but not for the relatives left behind.

After a sleepless night, Sunday came and first, I had to tell Rowan, our youngest daughter, who was seventeen. It was a massive shock for her too, but we had to leave her with her other grandparents in Dereham, a few miles outside of Norwich, as we had to go to Peterborough. They, too, were shocked to hear our news.

We drove to the police station in Bretton, mainly in silence. The police took us to the hospital, where I had to see Dad in the mortuary. They had done what they could to cover him, and there was a red rose on the blanket, but I cannot describe that memory any further. It lives with me every day though the pain has lessened.

Afterwards, we returned to Dad's house, and the silence was eerie. He was not there and would never be again. It all became a bit of a blur after that.

Firstly, I had to call my sisters, who were all abroad then. But, of course, due to the time differences and the fact they lived on USAF bases, it was difficult to get hold of them. So, the Red Cross initially contacted them, and got them to call me on Dad's number. Then I called our daughter Stephanie at University. Those were tough phone calls, and a round of other calls followed.

We stayed at Dad's house for a few hours and then returned home to Norwich for me to collect a few things. I had to return to Dad's house to await my sisters, who were joining me to help deal with everything that had to be done. We stayed in the house for two weeks arranging the funeral and sorting the house out, too, as time was short for all of us. Finally, the house had to be given back to the council. It was a strange and bittersweet time, as we all had to go our separate ways afterwards.

When all had been completed, I went back to Norwich as I had to eventually return to work, although my employer was understanding. It was still very difficult for the next six months as I had been appointed executor and had to deal with all of Dad's estate. This was a trial as I had to carry on as though nothing had happened in the world, but looking back, it was certainly an experience.

I never thought I would be able to write about this sad time, but now I believe it has helped me to cope with the memory.

Chapter Fourteen

Nellie Dean – Paternal Grandmother

My paternal grandmother was Ellen Isobel Russell, formerly Dean. The third eldest daughter of seven children of my great grandmother, Maria Dean, who lived to be 100. Grandma was known as Nell or Nellie by her family, being short for Ellen. She was born in 1894 in Mile End in East London. She died in approximately 1982, but I'm not sure of the date.

Grandma in 1913

One of the most important things about her was that she, like her mother, Maria, who was known as Tiny in the family, was very small in stature. She was probably under five feet tall, and when I was a teenager, I remember when I hugged her, saying, 'You are so small, Grandma.' But also, like her mother, she had a big personality.

49

Grandma wore a built-up surgical shoe all her life due to a fall when aged three, but because she never went to hospital to get it treated, the bone stopped growing properly leaving her with one leg three-inches shorter than the other. Conscious of this, Grandma would hide it behind her other leg in photographs.

Grandma in 1935

I remember an old worn-out pair that she used to wear around the house, like her slippers, and another shiny pair with a big button on the strap that she wore for going out.

Grandma always looked nice when she went out, which was rarely, and she always wore a hat and had a lovely brooch on her coat, a trait I think I have learnt from her, especially now I am older.

She told us that when she was eighteen, her waist measured nineteen inches, and in the photographs, you can see she was quite slim. As I remember, she was bigger but not overweight when she was older.

Grandma married at about twenty to my grandfather, Fred(erick) Alfred Russell. He was in the Merchant Navy as a steward all their married life apart from when he was a soldier in the Great War of 1914-18. Apart from that period, he was away at sea most of the time. She told us he had only been at home about six times for any period in all the years they were married, which was a long time.

Because of this, she became an independent lady and used to do everything in the home and the running of it, including cobbling hers and the children's shoes.

They had three children. Olive, born in 1916, Ronald (Ron),

born in 1918 and Fred, my dad. He was born in 1923. They lived in Old Ford Road, a part of Mile End, for a number of years.

After the Second World War, when a lot of east London was bombed in the Blitz, they were moved to Dagenham, a then newish town where many council houses were built for people to be re-

housed. That is where I remember her living when I used to visit.

My grandfather Fred died when I was about six, and we lived in Singapore, where Dad was stationed. I know as Dad came home on his own on compassionate leave for the funeral. We always knew our grandma living on her own in Dagenham, and the house was filled with many things Grandad brought home from his travels at sea, especially her sideboard, which had these big carved wooden Japanese men and other small ornaments. She had a lovely, laminated fire screen from Japan in front of the unused fire in her front room. Her Singer treadle sewing machine was placed in front of the window, looking out to the street, where she would sit for many happy hours making and repairing household articles like sheets, pillowcases, and clothes. She was an expert seamstress and always wore an overall, like a housecoat, which had many patches on that she had repaired. When I visited with my parents and sisters, we loved to listen to her stories.

She told us about visits to the music hall with her sisters and family when she was younger and went out with my grandfather, probably before the Great War in the post-Edwardian period. She knew many popular songs from that era like, *Come into the garden Maud*, *Get me to the church on time*, *Burlington Bertie from Bow* and of course, *There's an old mill by the stream Nellie Dean*, which was her namesake.

The favourite story she told us was about when she went out once with our grandfather. She had a new black hat with feathers that were popular then, and they went to the music hall by tram.

On the way back, it rained a lot, and of course, her hat got very wet. She couldn't understand why people kept looking at her on the tram. It wasn't until she got home and looked in the mirror that she saw her face was covered in the black dye from the wet and drooping feathers of her new hat. She was not best pleased and told us many times about how she berated and scolded her soon-to-be husband, who did not tell her this had happened. He obviously didn't think it important, but being a woman, she did.

Grandma in 1961 as I remember her

In her garden, there was an air raid shelter which we used to play on top of, as it was covered in lots of growth and weeds. She couldn't garden very well due to her foot, but she did have horseradish growing at the end of the plot, and I remember her and my mum used to pull it and make their own horseradish sauce when we used to visit. The smell was powerful and used to fill the house.

We loved visiting Grandma. She had a telephone, which was a great luxury in the days of the 1960s. We used to play with it sometimes as it was a great novelty to us. She was the only one in the family who had a phone, a reminder of the days when she was on her own, I expect, when her husband was at sea.

She told us she had had a good life, and although a little incapacitated by her disability, she never let it get her down or stop her from being a wonderful grandma to us all, seven grandchildren in all – and all girls too.

Chapter Fifteen

My Maternal Grandmother

My maternal grandmother, who we called our nannie, was born Kitty May Marsh in 3 High Street, Lewisham (London), on 26th March 1897.
She later married Ernest Albert Wallace, born in Romford in 1890. They were the proud parents of ten children, who were:
May Ruth born in 1919
Evelyn Joyce born in 1922 – my mother
Ernest William born in 1926
Leslie Albert born in 1928 and only lived a few months
Dorothy Kathleen born in 1929
Kitty Rose born in 1931
Joan Doreen born in 1932
Betty Eileen born in 1934
Sydney Albert born in 1936
John Henry born in 1938 (known as Bibby as he was the baby of the family).
   My mother Joyce told my sisters and me they were poor growing up as they did in the 1920s and 30s when there was the Depression, and many times they had little, not even shoes. Times were hard for them, and with such a big family, it was a struggle, but because of

53

Above: Nannie and Grandpa Wallace

this, they were very close. My mum told us our nannie fed her big family from a massive stewpot kept on the stove for days at a time, and which she kept filling up with as many bits of vegetables as she could find.

I remember my nannie lived in what seemed quite a big house at 18 Meadow Road in Rush Green, Romford, Essex. It was a council house and is still there today. It seemed bigger as I was a small child, but most of her family still lived at home then, so there must have been lots of room, or it seemed that way.

We didn't see her often as our dad was in the RAF from when I was two, and we lived far from Romford. My mum told me we used to visit her on the bus when we lived in Basildon, but I don't remember. However, when I was a bit older and returned to the UK from Singapore in 1963, we stayed with her for a few months at 18 Meadow Road. We stayed with my other Grandma Nell in Dagenham later. Because I was six or seven years old and had to attend school, I remember my nannie taking me and collecting me from the local infants' school and walking beside her, holding her hand and talking.

Another memory is being in her house and playing near the piano in one of the rooms. It was an upright one and had ornaments on the closed top. One of them was a Japanese lady, a gift from my parents from Singapore, now in my doll's cabinet collection. The cabinet was once Nannies in the corner of that house too.

One Christmas in the early 60s after we had returned from Singapore when my family were all there at Nannie's house. Nannie made us all sit together on the settee, and she gave us all snowballs of cottonwool that she and all the mums had made for us children (as we were then) to open as there were little gifts inside. Not much or expensive, but that is what we remember most of those special days – being together with our extended family.

As she had a lot of children, it means I have a lot of cousins. There are eighteen of us that were all our nannie's grandchildren, and I am the eldest girl, with my cousin Tony being the eldest boy. Unfortunately, her husband Ernest, our grandfather, died before I was born, and none of us except Tony really remember him. We had a very close relationship as cousins, but as the years have gone by, we don't, unfortunately, see each other much anymore, but when we do, we are always close again.

Nannie with Lee, Debra and Cousin Christine as babies

Eventually, when Nannie's children left her home and had their own homes and families, she left the old house in Rush Green and moved in with her namesake daughter, our Auntie Kitty. Sadly, Aunt Kit didn't have any children, but she took care of Nannie in her later years. They lived in a flat near the old gas works in Hornchurch, and I remember seeing it when we visited. Nannie developed severe arthritis in her older years, and Kit took care of her to the end. Nannie died in 1972 or 1973 when I was seventeen, but we were living in Germany as a family when Dad was stationed there, so we never saw the end. Although I was not close with my nan, she is always remembered with love and affection.

Here are a few photos of Nannie and family members:

Vicki Makins

Nannie, me, Cousin
Ray and Cousin
Tony on the blanket.

Mum walking out in Romford with
her parents, Kitty and Ernest Wallace.

**Above: The family altogether at the Riviera
Lido holiday camp in Bognor Regis in 1966.**

Chapter Sixteen

A Newsworthy Day

This newspaper print is from the Ilford Recorder and other newspapers on 1st August 1961. Local papers to where my family lived in East London.

It shows my paternal great-grandmother celebrating her 100th birthday when she was in hospital. She is with the mayor. I think it is newsworthy as not many people reach this grand old age.

The other photo shows her surrounded by her family, including four of her daughters. My grandmother is second from the right sitting down. I am not there as I was a tiny girl living in Singapore with my family at the time.

I do not remember her

A century old this week, Mrs. Maria Dean, of Manor Park, blows out the candles on her birthday cake, helped by the Mayor of East Ham, Councillor W. Chapman.

Mayor was at her 100th birthday

much, but of course have been told a lot about her, especially by my grandmother, who was one of her daughters. My great-grandmother was called Maria, but she was always known as Tiny or Tine as she was only 4 feet 2 inches. She was born in Stepney in London's old East End in 1861, and her maiden name was Perry.

In August 1883, she married Joseph Dean in a tiny church in Bow in East London. Whilst much of the surrounding area and buildings she would have known are no longer there now, the church is, and it is surrounded by roads and modern buildings.

Her husband Joseph, my great grandfather, was a tailor, and they had seven children together. These were Ada, Ellen (who was known as Nell – my grandmother), Rose, Lillian (Lil), Florence (Flo), and Joseph Junior and Thomas.

As well as these offspring, she brought up two of her sibling's children from a young age. These were nieces, Amelia and May. In addition to her own brood of seven, there were nine children altogether. I studied the censuses of 1901, and they lived at 101 Coutts Road, in Stepney, which was in the Mile End old town. Twelve people were living in their small, terraced house in East London at that time.

Her husband, Joseph Dean, who I never knew, worked hard in his trade but only lived until he was forty-six. Maria, widowed for over fifty-five years, brought up the family by herself. No mean feat in the days of no welfare state or help. It seems she may have been small in stature but was full of strength.

Many years later, when she was quite a bit older and all the family had left home, she moved in with her eldest daughter, Ada, who had been widowed when her husband (Bert Brittain) was killed after a bomb fell in their back garden during the Blitz. Much of east London was bombed during the Second World War, and Great-Grandma and Aunt Ada (who I knew her as) moved to a flat in East  Ham, where I remember her from.

When we visited our grandma in Dagenham when my sisters and I were small, the family went to see them in East Ham, and I remember jolly times. Our grandma would often tell us years later of the times when they had a singsong around the piano, which was there. They were lovely memories.

The strongest memory I have of *Tine* is when I was about three. She had recently broken her hip after a fall and had a crutch to help after the repair. I remember trying to use the crutch as a stilt.

Not long after that, we moved to Singapore in late 1958. She died three years later after celebrating her 100th birthday in hospital. A truly newsworthy day.

Chapter Seventeen

A Memorable Walk

We moved to Saltburn-by-the-Sea on April 4th, 2014. It had been a long journey from when we came here in 2013 to look at the place until that final day when we travelled here to live.

We had been up since three or four in the morning at our old house in Norwich, then drove for over five hours and came off the motorway near Stokesley. We had never been to this area on the way to Saltburn, and it looked pretty. Then as we travelled near Great Ayton, on our right came into view this very high hill, almost a mountain, with a strangely flat top. I said to Vic, my husband, 'I wonder what that is there?' It didn't seem to be on our road map either. It was the biggest hill we'd ever seen.

Later, once we had settled into our new home, we found out the high hill we had

Roseberry Topping

passed on our journey here was called *Roseberry Topping*. I discovered it had been known and named by the first Vikings settling in this part of the world in about 1119AD. They knew it as *Odin's Rock*.

When we got to know a few people around here, they told us that it is common for people to climb the tallest hill in Yorkshire, known as the *Matterhorn of the North*. It is 1,049 feet (320m) and on the Cleveland Way trail.

When six months had passed, come the September of 2014, we decided to attempt a walk to the summit of Roseberry Topping. It was a perfect day for the walk, with no wind or rain and reasonably warm.

We parked the car in the car park at Newton-under-Roseberry and set off. We had already noticed how there were often lots of cars there, so we knew it was a popular place for walking.

The path trail from the car park to the base of the hill was on the flat, and we enjoyed sauntering on this aspect of it. There was just Vic and I and our faithful companion, our dog, Bandit. We have had many walks together and enjoy the peace it brings.

On this occasion, we left the path once we reached the trees and started to steadily walk upwards. The trees are in a small wood at the base of the hill, and some tracks obviously veer to the incline. Not having been here before, we weren't sure which way to go but thought we'd keep heading upwards.

Eventually, once we left the trees, the path started to climb vertically. It became quite steep when we were about halfway between the base and the summit. There were a lot of loose stones and chippings too, and although we had our walking boots on, it could be quite slippery.

It was at this point I began to panic a bit. After a lifetime of little exercise and preferring a sedentary existence, a climb of this magnitude was quite a feat, especially as I don't like heights either. As we got higher, I was not keen on looking down where we had been. I remember particularly being amongst a lot of ferns and trying to find the path. When even Bandit, who is quite game at doing anything we ask him to, kept stopping as he didn't feel comfortable about climbing vertically, I knew this was not a good place to be. The worst moment for me was when I froze and suddenly felt petrified about going up the vertical incline. I said I didn't want to go on any further, and I just stopped in my tracks, almost crying. Vic, the stronger person in this situation and quite impatient, told me to stop being a wuss and to carry on. Our marriage stood another test at this point, as I knew he would have gone on without me, and I didn't really want to go back on my own. So, I breathed deeply and went for it.

With Vic's hand and Bandit waiting for me, we eventually reached the summit. I felt I had overcome a huge milestone, never mind about being at the top and looking at the wonderful views. You could even see the sea of Saltburn in the distance.

Once we had recovered, we sat against a rock at the summit and proceeded to eat the picnic we had brought. Whilst we sat there reflecting, a man came up just a little behind us, and we chatted. He told us he had been up Roseberry Topping at least fifteen times and saw this achievement as nothing more than a walk in the park. I thought it takes all sorts! When we told him about our journey up there that day, and he asked which way we had come, he told us we had gone up by way of the steepest side. No wonder it had been tough on us.

He told us which was the easiest way to go down, and needless to say, that was the route we took on our return journey a while later.

As he had confirmed, it made for a less arduous and easier route going down, and we were soon walking on a flatter surface on our way back to where the woods were at the base. I felt much better and pleased with myself for what I felt had been a massive achievement.

We have been past Roseberry Topping many times in recent years and been on a few walks around the base and in the woods. The bluebells in spring are particularly worth seeing. However, we haven't returned to the top, but I am glad I have achieved this as I remember it on that memorable day.

Chapter Eighteen

Stuck somewhere and a Childhood Incident

I have combined both subjects as they and the content fit together quite nicely, as you will see.

In 1983, we decided to have a holiday on the Isle of Wight, as we hadn't been there before. We booked into a Warners holiday camp, a smaller version of Butlins and Pontins more well-known ones. The holiday experience was still the same, including having the staff's childcare so the parents could have a break. The staff were identified by their green jackets and uniforms, as opposed to red and blue at Butlins and Pontins. Warners was later taken over by Haven Holidays, which now are mostly caravan parks. So, the summer holidays came, and it was not many weeks away until we were going.

Some two or three weeks before we went, Stephanie, our eldest daughter, went down with mumps, closely followed by the onset of chickenpox. She was six, and Rowan was four.

Stephanie was quite poorly but getting the two illnesses together wasn't a bad thing as it built up her immunity. Vic and I were frazzled and worried about it, but we were hopeful we could still go away as planned.

Rowan didn't seem to be showing any signs of either illness. After a visit to the doctor, when Stephanie was recovering, we were told it was probably all right to still go away. We duly packed up the car and set off from Norwich for Portsmouth, where we were to get the ferry to the Isle of Wight. We had a lovely journey down, and it was nice to be getting away.

We arrived at the Warners holiday camp at Puckpool, near Yarmouth, and had a lovely week. We took the girls to Blackgang Chine, a great tourist attraction for children, and visited Osborne House, the home of Queen Victoria and Prince Albert, which I loved.

When we weren't out, we stayed in the camp and had a lovely time as there were always many activities to keep us all busy. The girls were fine with the green coats, and we felt relaxed after a lovely holiday. Then on the last night, Rowan didn't appear to be well. She kept complaining of an earache and was most unhappy. I remember sitting in the ballroom with her on my lap, trying to comfort her and later dosing her with children's paracetamol.

After a restless night, we packed and loaded the car, ready to return home. We had booked to go on the 12pm ferry. We went to the camp dining room to have our last breakfast there, and Rowan seemed to have perked up a bit. But children being what they are, the craving to go play began when they had finished their food, and we let them go to the play area but said to be careful.

Just as we were leaving the table, one of the staff came and told us there had been an accident. Rowan had fallen off the climbing frame in the play area, which was thankfully sited on bark chippings, but she had bumped her head. Oh my God! As you can imagine, we were in a state when we went to find the children.

When I picked up Rowan, she had a great egg-shaped bump on her forehead, but I noticed a few red spots on her neck and chest. The onset of chickenpox, of course. It had been just over two weeks since Stephanie had it, so it must have been incubating, and I expect the earache was part of it. We were then told that someone had called for an ambulance to take Rowan for a hospital check-up due to the fall and the quite bad bump on her head.

By this time, Vic and I were in bits and in panic mode because we were due to catch the ferry at 12pm, and our chalet had all been cleared out, ready for the next batch of visitors. What were we to do?

I went with Rowan to the hospital in Yarmouth in the ambulance, and Vic had to explain to the reception staff at the camp. We knew by this time that Rowan would be kept in overnight for twenty-four hours observation, and of course, I was staying with her in the guest room. Warners couldn't have been more helpful as they gave Vic and Stephanie another chalet to stay in at no extra charge. Unfortunately, we had to cancel our ferry trip, but the Warners reception told us they would sort it out for us in due course when we could leave, which we appreciated too.

This was helpful as, by this time, they and all the hospital staff concerned knew that our daughter had early onset chickenpox. She had quite a few more spots developing by the hour. Consequently, she was put into an isolation room on the children's ward.

This is the part of that time we remember the most as the poor paramedics in the ambulance were not best pleased when they learnt of the chickenpox. First, they had to fumigate the ambulance after we'd left, then later the isolation ward she was in. We learnt the next day before we left to go home that a couple of the green coat staff had gone down with the spots too. Fortunately, Rowan did not suffer any ill effects after her fall.

We look back on this time and our unexpected stay and laugh now, but it wasn't funny then. Even when we managed to get another ferry the next day, on explaining what had happened and about the trip to the hospital, it seemed the ferry people couldn't get us off the island quickly enough.

That journey home was one of the fastest ones we had done. I'm pleased to say Rowan was ok afterwards, and children are resilient.

This experience leaves us with a mixed memory of that holiday on the Isle of Wight.

The holiday camp at Puckpool is now closed but was used in the cult movie *That'll Be the Day* in 1972, starring David Essex and Ringo Starr.

Chapter Nineteen

A Memorable Trip

I have had many memorable and great trips over the years, but the one I will write about here is when we went to Okinawa, an island part of the Prefecture (a subdivision) of Japan. This was in October 1998.

We visited one of my sisters, Lee, stationed there on a USAF base with her husband, Luke and their two girls, Lauren and Lynn.

It was memorable for many reasons, and the first was because this trip took place about eighteen months after my sisters, and I, had suddenly lost our dad. After the traumatic events we shared in January 1997, we all had to go our separate ways, which was hard on us.

Lee had come and gone the furthest, travelling from Okinawa, and I decided when I had finished doing Dad's estate, as his executor, that I would use some of the inheritance he had left me to go and visit Lee and her family. In some ways, I felt I was doing it for him, but also, it would be nice to meet Lauren and Lynn for the first time, who were eight and six, respectively.

So began our trip. We went to see a travel agent in Norwich, who helped us plan and sort it out. We would have to change planes four times to cut down the cost. Also, it was not the sort of place people generally went to for their holidays.

The only people in Okinawa, besides the local Japanese population, were USAF servicemen. It was home to bases the military had held since the 2nd World War when it was heavily involved. My brother-in-law was stationed there for four years.

We left on the 4th of October 1998 from Norwich airport to Schipol in Amsterdam, where we landed about an hour later.

We travelled with China Airlines, and all our bags were labelled from Norwich to land at Naha airport – the small airport on Okinawa Island. We didn't see them until we arrived – it was all very efficient.

At that time, Vic and I were smokers, and of course, we had waited until we got to Amsterdam to get our duty-free at the airport. As we smoked roll-ups, we bought tobacco from the shops and carried it in our hand luggage. We didn't think about what the consequences could turn out to be.

We boarded the plane from Amsterdam to Taipei, which is in Taiwan. This first part of the trip was sixteen hours long, and then we landed at Bangkok airport in Thailand, where the plane had to refuel. We waited about three hours and only had time to spend at the airport. We found many strange and different sights and sounds there, the culture being different from ours. I particularly remember seeing the signs saying *Drug smuggling is punishable by death,* which was a shock. Still, at least the authorities dealt with drug use properly.

After the waiting time, we boarded the plane again bound for Taiwan. We had about a four-hour journey and then arrived in Taipei when it was evening. The travel schedule told us there was only one plane daily to Naha airport in Okinawa. However, it went the following day, so we were put up in a hotel near Taipei airport. The Chang Kai Sek hotel was part of China Airline's service. It was excellent, and all the people serving us were most hospitable.

We were given a room at the top of a tall building, as most of them were, and it was nice to have some time to bath and relax after our already long journey.

The meal we had was memorable too. We went to the hotel

dining room, where a big buffet had been laid on for the guests, and it looked wonderful though we weren't sure what most of the food was. However, it was ok apart from when I tried what looked like pieces of mandarin oranges dipped in a sugary coating. Instead of sweet as I expected them to be, they were fiery hot and nearly blew my mouth away. They had been dipped in a chilli sauce, which was burning hot. I shall never forget that experience.

The next day, we boarded the plane to Naha. The final stage of our long trip was good, especially as we found out as we left Taipei that a typhoon hit there soon after. It was just under two hours to get to Naha, and I remember vividly looking out of the windows at the sea below and seeing the island coming into view. It was a small, light aircraft with few passengers on it. We were the only white English people there, and many men dressed in uniform from an athletic club were travelling for an event. Also, there were a lot of retired Japanese war veterans who were travelling to a reunion in Okinawa.

We landed at Naha and had a terrible experience because the tobacco we bought at Amsterdam airport was thought to be drugs, and the officials searched through our cases. We were questioned most ferociously, and the Japanese authorities showed us pictures of drugs as they didn't speak English, nor did we know their language. We had fingers pointed at us, which was awful, and they even had dogs at one point. It was terrifying.

When they realised we were innocent tourists and let us go through the green OK door, we were the only people left as all the other passengers had passed through already.

It was a great relief when we went through the exit doors to find Lee and Luke waiting. They were worried something had happened to us as we had been held up for such a long time.

We were really pleased to see them, and they took us back to their home for the start of a wonderful holiday, where we had time with them and were introduced to their daughters.

We stayed for over two weeks and had a great time and holiday, but that is another story.

Chapter Twenty

A Most Frightening Experience

After our memorable trip to Okinawa in October 1998, we went on to have a wonderful holiday with my sister and her family.

They took us to some amazing and different places, like the Tropical Gardens, a Sea Life Centre, a Snake Farm – where they were highly venomous – and traditional Japanese dancing in a theatre. We were well looked after and had some lovely meals out. Then, a few days into the holiday, they told us they had a surprise for us. They had booked us all to go to a resort called Okuma, on the other side of the island, so we would have to spend a couple of days there. It was a resort owned by the USAF, and personnel could spend vacation time there when off duty.

In the middle weekend of staying there, Luke and Lee drove us all to Okuma, and we stayed in a sort of chalet called a cabana. It had all mod cons and was just yards from the beautiful sandy beach in a lovely tropical bay.

We spent some time on the beach swimming in the sea amid the clear blue waters. Even in October in the Far East, it was warm, about 80 deg F. After a while, and I can't remember whose idea it was, it was decided that we would go out for a ride on the banana boat, making trips from the shore edge. We had watched from a distance – it seemed to be a lot of fun, and people enjoyed going out on it.

We went to the office to book for later in the afternoon. When we returned, we had to try on life jackets and have a safety talk. I should have known then it was not going to be a good idea.

So, our time came. The boat came to the shore edge, and we all got on the banana boat floats. I was in the middle section with our two nieces, Lauren and Lynn. Of course, being young and having no fears, they were excited, but they knew I wasn't keen. Lynn (aged six) said, 'Don't worry, Auntie Vicki, we'll look after you.' It was nice but not reassuring.

The banana boat floats were attached with a long rope affair to a small boat, which, once we were all astride, didn't waste time setting off. It seemed to go very fast, and all I could do was cling on for dear life.

We went a few yards from the shore, and then we went further out into what to me was the open sea. The banana floats bobbed and bobbed, and we went up and down on them like riding a horse.

Then the man in the boat turned to do a semi-circle, and the floats started to go sideways.

I was quite scared then, but before I knew what had happened, the floats had begun to tip, and that was it. We had all been thrown off and were in the sea. We went quite a few feet under the water; it was deep, and I was petrified. I thought this was it – I'll drown, but I was thinking about the rest of the family, especially the girls who were so small.

I had never been in such deep water before, but I thanked God for the life jackets as, of course, we floated to the surface in what seemed like a long time but was probably only seconds.

When I came up, I was gasping and couldn't get my breath, but it was from fright and terror, not anything else. Then I saw the boat

71

a little further away from us, and he turned round to pick us up. My sister Lee swam over to me as she could see the state I was in. I was almost hysterical, and she had a job to help me to the boat, with the man pushing out long poles to grab onto. I can't explain the feeling of relief when the boat was near, and the man forcefully pulled me and helped me into it. To be out of the deep water was all I wanted, and I did not think of my dignity then.

Once I was over my shock, I found out if everyone was ok and checked if the girls were safe too. Back in the boat, it became clear that I was the only one who had acted like a *wuss*, but I didn't care. Everyone else had enjoyed it but not me.

We have talked about that experience many times over the years, and I don't think my sister and I will ever forget it.

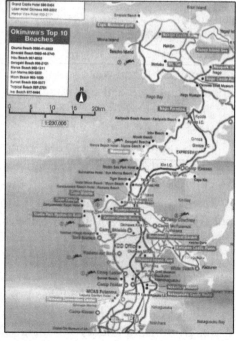

Chapter Twenty-One

A Joyful Journey

This joyful journey occurred in approximately October 1962 when I was almost seven and my sisters Lee and Debra were four. We lived at RAF Odiham in Hampshire and had not long moved there after our dad's tour of Singapore finished. The weather was different here from the tropical heat we had been living in for the past three years. To keep us warm in the autumn and winter of that year, our mum had bought us children a pair of tartan trousers or *trews* as she called them. My sisters and I still remember them even now after all these years. We all had them in different tartan colours and wore them when we went out in the colder weather and felt cosy in them too.

When it was late September or early October that year, we all went to stay with our grandma in Dagenham, Essex. Perhaps it was for half term, but I can't really remember. However, I recall seeing Grandma and being excited to stay at her house as we didn't see her very often. On the second night, we were all put to bed a bit earlier than usual, and nothing seemed any different. But after a couple of hours, a great surprise happened. Mum and Dad came in and woke us up to tell us they had a treat for us as we had all been good. We were going out on a special journey in the car.

I cannot describe how strange this was for us three little girls to be woken from our beds, told to get out of our pyjamas, put on our warm tartan trews and a warm jumper and shoes, and to be going out in the dark. The memory has stayed with me, and it was a wonderful experience as we didn't know where we were heading.

Mum and Dad finally explained we were going to see the lights at Southend after many excited questions from us. Of course, we weren't any the wiser as we had never experienced anything like this before. However, even after being woken from our sleep early, it was still a fantastic adventure. You can imagine how thrilled we were when we saw the lights for the first time as we approached Southend.

Southend-on-Sea is one of the nearest seaside places to Dagenham, which is very inner-city just in the east of London. The lights there are as famous in Essex as the Blackpool lights, although perhaps not as big but still attract people even nowadays.

It was truly magical – the colours, and the twinkling, flashing lights. I remember many designs and models in lights like coaches, animals, and trees. Like Christmas about four times over.

We watched it through the car window with our faces pressed to the glass. It was amazing. Then Dad parked the car, and we walked along the promenade to see the lights up close. We were enthralled by it all and thrilled to see everywhere looking magical.

We eventually returned to the car and were told that because it was getting late, we would have to return to Grandma's. The evening didn't end there, though, as we stopped at a fish and chip shop on the front, and Mum got out to get us all a late supper, whilst not forgetting to take home a piece of skate wing for Grandma, which she loved. Because she was housebound, this was a real treat for her. I expect it was for Mum and Dad, after being in the tropical climate and in a different culture too.

We returned to her house, and all sat in the living room eating the fish and chips out of newspaper. It was a lovely ending to our surprise *journey of joy*. Despite seeing beautiful light displays over the years, especially at Christmas, this joyful journey when we were very young is the one I remember most.

Chapter Twenty-Two

Teachers I Have Known

I have known many teachers in my younger life, having been to many different schools, and I have written about this in another chapter.

The following are the people who have affected my life or memory.

Mr Goult & Miss Parrott – These were the only two teachers at the Syderstone V C Primary school my two sisters and I went to between 1964 and 1967.

It was located in the village of Syderstone, outside the camp of RAF Sculthorpe in Norfolk, where we lived at the time. The camp primary school was not open for the first few years we lived there, so we had to go to the school in the nearest village.

It was almost a two-mile walk from our house and in all weathers, as there was no transport, and our mum didn't drive – walking was our only option. Being the oldest (and about nine), I was in charge of taking care of my sisters to get there and back each day.

In school, I was in Mr Goult's class for the older pupils, and Lee and Debra were in Miss Parrott's class, where she took the younger pupils from the reception year to about eight years of age. There were not many children in the whole school.

I was all right in Mr Goult's class, and he was fine. I remember he was a slightly rotund older man wearing tweed suits with a waistcoat. I look back on the teaching he did for me and others with fondness as I learnt a lot and enjoyed being there too. Going into a school in Norfolk was a new experience, as we had recently moved there, and it was all strange.

Miss Parrott was, however, a different person altogether. If she had been around today, she would certainly have been struck off from the teaching profession. I did not have her as my teacher, but I heard about her from my sisters. Really, they should write this as their memories would be more valid, but this is what I know – she was old even to us small girls then, and she had been a teacher at the school for years. Probably one of those who had never been to a teacher's training school as they weren't around in her younger days. Unlike nowadays in the teaching profession, she probably had no formal qualifications either.

She was hard and cruel, and we found out in later years she had even put so-called *naughty* children in a cupboard and left them there for a couple of hours. Imagine the fright this had on young and impressionable children.

She walked with a stick, the result of a former pupil having thrown a stone at her outside school hours, which caused her leg to be injured. This image made her even more witch-like than she already was.

My sisters were frightened of her. They were only five or six at the time, remember? So, on a Monday morning, their class did *what we did at the weekend* exercise, and my mum used to write on a note for them to look at as they were too scared to recall anything.

The worst incident was the day Debra asked to go to the toilet. Although she had put up her hand a few times and been ignored, Miss Parrott finally refused to let her go from the classroom to the loos outside. Needless to say, the inevitable happened, and my poor sister had an accident.

I was called out of my class by Mr Goult to take Debra home. We had no phone, and there were no mobiles then, and nothing else could be done. I cannot even describe the trauma this incident caused. Not only had my little sister messed herself, but she and I had to walk home on a cold day with her in a terrible state and crying, of course. Even today, my sister is still affected by this event when we talk of those days.

When we arrived home, our mum went nuts and was soon at the school to complain about Miss Parrott. I am sure there were lots of apologies, and *it won't happen again,* but it shouldn't have happened in the first place.

If Miss Parrott had been here today, she would have been found guilty of cruelty to children.

It was sometime after this that the school on the RAF camp opened, and Lee and Debra moved away from Miss Parrott and her horrible bullying ways, and they were much happier.

I stayed on at the school for a little longer than them as I was due to take the eleven plus exams, which I did and then duly went onto the grammar school in nearby Fakenham.

Mrs Bagnall – In 1967, I attended Fakenham Grammar School, now the High, for three years. Again, it was a totally new experience as it was much bigger and had many more pupils.

I made a few new friends and enjoyed the lessons immensely as I loved learning and still do.

The teacher I remember particularly from then was Mrs Bagnall, or *Baggy* as we called her. She took me for needlework.

She was the only teacher there for DS (domestic science) and needlework. Of course, only the girls took these subjects in those days whilst the boys did woodwork and other skills of a practical nature.

We did needlework for the first to third years and then changed to DS in the years after that, but I wasn't there then, so I never learnt cooking at school.

She was a good teacher but strict, and I did learn a lot. What I remember most about her is coming into class, having to line up with the other girls, and having our skirts measured using a long, upside-down ruler. Due to the fashions of the time, this was the *swinging sixties*, short skirts were the in thing, however, not for school. As we wore maroon gymslips with a pleated skirt, it was difficult to wear them short, but we rolled them at the waist over our house belts. They must have looked silly, but we didn't think it at the time. We were measured as the skirts had to be the regulation two inches below the knee, and we were told off if they weren't.

My time ended there in 1970 after I moved to Germany when Dad was posted there. Starting at Windsor Girls' School with my sisters was the next chapter of my school days. There I met many interesting teachers, but that is for another time.

Chapter Twenty-Three

Places I Have Lived and Windsor Girls' School

I have mentioned briefly in other chapters about my time at Windsor Girls' School, the boarding school I attended in Germany. I spent three memorable years there with my two sisters, Lee and Debra.

We were sent there from 1970-73 as there was no secondary school on the RAF camp where our dad was stationed. As the other choices were school in the UK (which our parents couldn't afford), a local German school, or no school at all (which some opted to do), the final option was to go to a boarding school. These were part of the BFES (British Forces Education Service) system. Numerous schools were set up, such as Kings School, Queens, Prince Rupert and others, across West Germany. These were to cater for the children of personnel in the RAF and Army stationed there. We went to Windsor Girls' School in Hamm, BFPO 103.

Getting there – As Hamm was quite some distance from where we lived in Weeze, a German village just outside the base of RAF Laarbruch, we had to travel to school on the train. The RAF and Army paid for much of the travel to our school and the other BFES schools dotted around West Germany. On our first day, we were driven by our parents to the nearest station, the Bahnhof in Goch, a nearby town. The excitement and nervousness of myself and my two sisters was at fever pitch. This, of course, did help to cope with leaving and saying goodbye to our loved ones.

We were amazed by how many other pupils and families were at

the station in readiness. As it was compulsory to travel in school uniform, it was a sea of black blazers with the *Concordia* crest on – the school's motto – and girls in red berets, and of course, the boys who were going to the neighbouring Windsor Boys' School. Seeing so many people with guitars amongst their luggage surprised me too.

I remember sharing a carriage with a Laarbruch boy who had been at the school for a while. He told us stories about what went on there. He played tunes on his guitar as we travelled. Looking back, it was like a scene from the Harry Potter books, as they describe making their way to Hogwarts.

Arriving there – After a couple of hours of travelling, we reached Hamm station, where buses waited to take us to the schools, and we arrived at the gates of WGS, our home for the next three years.

I was a 4th year, and my sisters were in the 1st year. We already knew we were in Edinburgh house, and that is where we were dropped off. The school

The entrance was forbidding – even in 'our' time.

grounds were large and all fenced off. Some fences had barbed wire at the top. They were buildings set up in a sort of rectangular fashion, very military-like as they had been former German barracks with cavalry stables during the Second World War. The British Army later used them as a tank division when it was housed by Newcastle barracks. It was near the barracks of Munster, where the British Army was still sited. The BFES took over it all, and it

Windsor School in May 1954 with a close up of 'Peg Leg' Block, later occupied by Edinburgh and Balmoral.

was opened as a school in 1953.

The buildings were set up as follows: There was a big field beside the main buildings, and alongside this housed the sickbay and a large gymnasium. A long road went around this area which we later found out was called the *einbahnstrasse*, or one-way system. This led to the chapel, where we attended with our own Padre, who taught at school. We came here every Sunday and for special occasions such as Remembrance Sunday and Christmas.

We arrived at Edinburgh House. The building was shared with the

house Balmoral on the bottom two floors, and Edinburgh was on the top two. Of course, there were no lifts and many stairs to climb. We were greeted by our Matron, who was German, as all the non-teaching staff were. Frau Schroeder was her name, and she ruled with a rod of iron. Discipline was her middle name, as we soon found out.

As I was in 4th year, I was allocated a dormitory with two other girls from my year. The dorms were individually made up of six beds for the 1-3rd years, respectively, and three bed or two bed for the 4th-6th years. You did not necessarily know the girls you shared with and could request to share with friends as you were there for longer and got to know people, but it was hard at first to share with strangers. We had a Head of House, and she had her own room, being about eighteen at the time. Respect was shown to her as she was usually one of the eldest of us.

There were large bathrooms and shower cubicles on each floor. In addition, the House Mistress, in each house, had her own flat at the end of one of the corridors, and the Matron had her own room for when she was with us, or she could go back to her own home at the end of her shift. As we were at the top of the building, we had access to the attics of the house, where we regularly held our house meetings.

This leads me to remember what we were told about the presence of Pegleg. On our first few nights at the school, to make things even worse, being away from home for the first time, there was sometimes a loud banging coming from the attics above us. New girls were told this was Pegleg. The ghost of an airman who had crashed into the barracks during the Second World War.

It seemed possible at the time and was quite scary as you often heard the banging. But, later, it was realised this was probably older girls up there making the noises for fun.

Settling In – After the first day in the House, the school day began. This was with bells.

The first one was the rising bell at 7am, and it was at 8am at weekends as we were allowed an extra hour in bed.

Then we had to get washed and dressed in our school uniforms to be ready to line up at 7.20am, signified by a bell. It was always a bit of a rush to find a space in the bathroom, but Matron had devised a timetable for baths and showers, which was pinned to the walls of the bathrooms. So, usually, by dorm, we had to follow the timetable, and some girls would have been allocated perhaps an early shower or bath before breakfast. As there were probably fifty to sixty girls per house, it was quite a feat of organisation, but we managed somehow.

Then we lined up, ready for the first trip of the day, which was to the dining hall for breakfast. This was from 7.30-8.30, and all the girls in the school and some teachers were there. We were eight to a table of mixed ages from all years and served by German waiting staff. The cooks were German too.

The food was good, and we had lots of choices, but beans on French toast was always the favourite in the mornings. After breakfast, we went back to the House to prepare for school, after making the bed and a general tidy up.

It was bells again for roll call first at about 8.40am. This was done every day and again in the evening later. Then we walked to the school block.

School began at 9am, and lessons were divided by more bells, as in most schools. Break was at 10.45, approximately – bell, to the dining room for tea, buns or biscuits. Lessons again at about 11am by the bell.

Bells again for lunch at 12.30-1.30 in the dining room, then back to the house for ten minutes to rest on beds, then bell again for 1.40 for line-up. Then walk back to school block for the 2pm bell for afternoon lessons. Bells until school ended at 3.30pm.

Then back to the house for break and catching up time until bell and line-up for tea at 4pm to the dining hall. This consisted of tea, sandwiches and cakes. After tea, it was back to the house again for a little free time for us all and homework for the younger pupils for a couple of hours until the bell went for supper at 6pm. Another line-up and off to the dining room for our last cooked meal of the day. After supper, the younger pupils went back to house for free time and washing until bedtime. The 4th and 5th years went to the gym for Prep for two hours or more, where we were supervised by teachers on duty. We followed a quite strict timetable as we were preparing for our GCEs by then, but it did not stop us from having fun sometimes too.

The 6th form girls had much more time to themselves and were expected to be stricter. After our Prep time, we went back to the house to get ready for bed, and there was a set time for each age-related dorm for lights out.

Privs – During this time, we weren't allowed out of school uniform until bedtime, except for two hours on a Saturday and Sunday afternoons.

Saturday mornings after breakfast were spent doing homework or Prep for the 4th to 6th years in the gym for two hours. The 1st - 3rd years did their washing, had free time, or did some tidying before lunch. We had to do our own washing of smalls and any other delicate items, for which we had to bring our own laundry bags from home. The bigger items and sheets went to the laundry each week, and we had to change our bedding weekly.

After our lunch break and bells, we were finally allowed out of the school for the first time all week for two hours. This was called *Privs* or privileges. Beforehand all the girls lined up outside the House Mistress's office to collect their pocket money sent in by their parents to cover the whole term. The House Mistress looked after it and kept a book to log it. For fairness, parents were told how much to send in advance, so no girl was allowed more than others in their year.

The 1st-3rd years had to go out accompanied by Matron, and the rest of us were allowed out by ourselves, but we had to go out in twos. Of course, we were out in our uniforms too, but if we stayed in or returned to the Houses, we could change into casual clothes for the rest of the day. That was one of the biggest treats, to relax in our jeans or own comfy clothes for a change.

We usually walked to the nearest park, the Kuhr park, where Matron often went with the younger girls. Or we went to the kiosk to buy sweets or other small treats. Unfortunately, we only were allowed into Hamm once a year, at the end of the Christmas term.

Of course, the downside of this treat was that if any of us were naughty, this privilege of going out and having pocket money was stopped. Also, many girls had brothers or boyfriends at the nearby Windsor Boys' school, and they met up with them then.

The Boys and Socials – So, the boys. We did not see that many of them as they were housed in their own school and buildings a little down the road. Thus, once a term, we had a *Social* as it was called.

Each year group from 1st - 5th had their own *Social,* which was held alternately at the boys' school and then the girls' school the following term.

The days leading up to the socials were a joy to us all, as they were the highlight of the school years. Many girls had brought their new clothes and outfits from home for the occasion. This was the 1970s, and the fashions were varied, trouser suits, mini and maxi dresses and, of course, hot pants for the girls and flares and kipper ties for the boys too.

The girls spent most of the Saturday afternoon of the social getting ready before supper, putting on makeup and styling each other's hair. It was definitely the *dress to impress* time, and I'm sure the boys, for their part, were no different.

The socials were held in the school hall and usually a group and disco music played. But, of course, there were teachers to keep an eye on us, and it was always lovely to see them in an informal setting for a change. It was fun to see them letting their hair down on the dance floor, and many a girl on Monday morning was pleased to brag they had a dance with their favourite teacher. In addition, it allowed gossiping about the socials for quite a while after.

When we went up to the Sixth form, we had the opportunity to go to the Admin Ball, which was a much more formal occasion.

Long dresses were the order of the day and suits for the boys, and again being the 1970s, many girls wore maxi dresses, as was the fashion. I attended one of these balls when I was in the Lower Sixth before I left the school, and it is a nice memory. I remember many girls having posh and probably expensive, formal gowns brought with them from shops in England. I, however, made mine. It was a pretty, purple material with tiny flowers, long sleeves, and a sweetheart neckline.

As we were the senior girls and boys at that time, we had a group of pupils playing from the boys' school. They were called *Durgy Grommit* and were very popular playing songs of the day. Their sound was from rock bands such as Deep Purple and Led Zeppelin. A good time was had by all, and I suppose today it would be likened to the Proms events that are now held in our schools.

Chapter Twenty-Four

My Working Life

I started my first paid job when I was fifteen. Before that, I had only ever been paid for babysitting for families. There were lots of opportunities for doing this job then as there were lots of young families on the RAF camps where we lived.

We moved to Germany in 1970, where Dad was stationed at RAF Laarbruch on the Dutch border. I went to a boarding school in Hamm, which I remember in this memoir, Windsor Girls' School.

On returning home for the holidays, I decided I wanted to do a part-time job as I was old enough. The school leaving age at that time was fifteen, and you could do a part-time job if still at school.

After advice from the Families Office on camp and my dad, I applied and received my National Insurance number to allow me to begin work. My first job was as a catering assistant/waitress in the Airmen's Mess on the camp. This was the canteen where the mainly single men in the RAF used to eat. Not only was it my first step into the world of work, but it introduced me to the opposite sex for the first time, as many of the men were relatively young and cheeky. It was a lot of fun. I did this job for about a year, on and off, and then went back to school in the in-between times as it was part-time, so I could fit it into the school holidays.

I had been assuming I could carry on this type of work each holiday, but then one Christmas, the Employment Officer on the camp, said there were no vacancies in the Airmen's Mess, but there were vacancies in the Officers' Mess, in their accommodation blocks.

This job was called a *Batwoman*, as opposed to a *Batman*, which are service expressions for a valet, which the men did.

Basically, it was a chambermaid or a *skivvy*, I'd call it now, as it entailed making the beds and cleaning and tidying the rooms of the RAF Officers in two blocks and the female teachers in the third block. These were teaching at the primary school on the camp, and this is where they lived.

I did the job with a couple of young teenage girls like me, and we were overseen by some Italian Matriarchs who worked there full-time. We were under the overall control of Frau Schaffer, who was like our German matron at school, a harridan and a force to be reckoned with.

As she had been there a long time, she had made herself indispensable to the officers taking on a lot of their extra work, such as ironing their RAF shirts (they had starched collars), thick trousers and cleaning their shoes.

However, the other girls and I did as little as we could as the job was boring and certainly an eye-opener when you saw how the other half lived. The rooms were usually a tip with things strewn everywhere. We had to tidy them up and clean whilst often getting scolded by the Italian ladies who didn't speak much English and probably swore at us in their own language. Being young then, we weren't too bothered about the standards required. We only wanted to be paid.

My part-time work in Germany ended in 1973 when we returned to England as Dad was posted back to Norfolk, where we had lived before. I was at a life crossroads then and didn't know what to do at first, and the only chance of work in the isolated camp where we lived was to go fruit picking on the land nearby as it is very rural. I decided to find a job for the long summer holiday that stretched ahead. The nearest town was Fakenham, which was eight miles away, and there was only one bus a week, and therefore not easy to get to.

I met a girl called Debbie at the camp, and we became friends. We saw a job advertised to work at Butlins in Clacton for the summer and went for an interview at Colchester. It was a big experience going by myself when I was seventeen on a train from King's Lynn.

We got jobs and soon went to Clacton for the summer season, working as a coffee bar assistant in one of the big coffee bars for the holidaymakers. Debbie got a job as a waitress working in the campers' dining hall.

It was a lot of fun, and we enjoyed meeting many people daily. It was hard work and hot too, but I did well there and was made a chargehand, giving me my first experience working on a till. But, of course, they weren't electronic in those days.

We worked six days a week with a day off, and if we completed our three-month contract, we got a bonus at the end, which was worth it in those days of the early 70s. Bed and Board and all meals were included, so it wasn't too bad, and I earned extra money by waitressing in the evenings for buffets when there was a Cabaret Show night for the campers. And there were tips.

It was a great time and a life learning curve as it was my first time working away from home. A lovely memory – especially as the Butlins camp at Clacton is no longer there. It was one of the first camps after the War and has been demolished.

When I returned home after the end of the summer, I went to King's Lynn College to do my A levels, and it was then I met Vic, now my husband of forty-five years.

After we were married, we moved to Norwich as I was due to start at what was then Keswick Hall Teachers Training College to train to be a primary school teacher.

However, I gave this up after a year, as I was expecting our eldest daughter, Stephanie. My tutor told me I could have continued my studies and placed her in the crèche, but I didn't want to do that. This was the 1970s, and it was quite the norm for women to have their families young and stay at home to look after them, and that is what I wanted to do.

So, I was at home for over ten years, and we had our youngest daughter Rowan during that time.

It was a tough and sometimes trying time being a stay-at-home mum, with only one wage coming in. Vic worked hard too, but on the whole, it was a good time, and I loved every minute of it with my lovely family. We were very happy. It is said it is the best time when your children are young. Looking back, it is certainly true.

Of course, when the girls were both at school, I realised the best time was over, and I decided to return to work. This was in 1986 and luckily, I managed to get a part-time job, in term-time only, at the local Technical College, working in catering again. I did this for three years, and it was a great help to me as a person, regaining my independence, and it helped to have extra money coming into the household too. I made many friends there too and enjoyed it overall, especially as it fitted in with my family's needs. After a while, though, and as the girls were becoming more and more able to look after themselves, the seeds of boredom began to set in again, and I started looking for a job where I could use my brain more. I had already decided not to go back and fulfil my teaching career. After being at home and having spent some time doing childminding for others and helping out in their playgroups and nursery schools, I felt I wanted a change from working with children.

Chapter Twenty-Five

My Favourite Job

After a few visits to the Job Centre in Norwich, I saw the advert for work required as a clerical assistant at Norwich Union. Now called *Aviva*, this was and still is one of the biggest employers in Norwich and has over 800 people working there and more employed in country-wide offices. They mainly deal with insurance products but have large departments which deal with pensions.

When I started working there, it was 1989, and there had been an explosion in the pension world. The government had changed the rules, and employees could join pension schemes and contract out of the State Earnings Related Pension Scheme. This meant their National Insurance contributions were paid into the company pension instead of one set up by the government. This brought in work for companies like NU. As they expanded their workforce, I was one of many accepted and started there in the summer of 1989. I was thirty-three with a family, and it was my first time working a full-time job since I had left school – it was all very strange, but the hours were classed as flexitime, which meant you did not have a set start and finish time. This fitted in well with family life.

This new job meant working on a computer, which I knew

At my desk in the office, 1998.

nothing about, but the training and the calibre of the more experienced people there who taught us were second to none. Because of this and the people I met and worked with there, meant it became my favourite job in my working life. I took to it like a duck to water and stayed there for over fifteen years. I became a pension administrator and learned a lot about financial services professionally. I took exams and passed my Financial Planning Certificate Part I, which is what some IFAs must take now. I really enjoyed the people side of the job, although I was in a back-office role but doing a lot of customer service on the phone.

We moved a lot to different offices in Norwich as the work became less or more, depending on the situation. NU has been in Norwich since the 1700s, as proven by the archives and museum held in their Marble Hall in the headquarters in Surrey Street. It is interesting if you could get to see it when it is open to the public.

Because of the moves, we used to do a lot of packing and unpacking of boxes to get settled into the various offices we were located to.

The first office I was in was at Sussex Street, not far from Anglia Square. It was a block of buildings next to the Spread Eagle pub, which was obviously well-visited at lunchtime by many of the staff. I remember particularly after entering the NU building that you came into a large atrium, which let all the light in through the roof. There were many comfortable chairs to sit on, which we did at lunchtime and during breaks from work.

NU provided all the staff with subsidised meals, and there was a restaurant and kitchen on-site with a huge array of hot and cold meals – the variety was immense. I thought this was amazing as I had never been employed in a place where people served me. I had stayed at home as a housewife or served on tables and cleared up after others. So, I enjoyed that.

As I mentioned, the company provided flexitime hours to fit work with your family life. This was another bonus, as both girls were now at secondary school, and I still had to be there for them. But if I could complete thirty-five hours a week, I could start and finish work at times I chose but had to be there between ten and three – the core hours, as they were the busiest.

I did all my training at Sussex Street; looking back, it was good, and I loved it. We worked in teams with a team leader, and it was very busy going on training courses and getting to know the work and the people. I was there for two years and then returned later when NU had one of their many swap rounds of the work from place to place, even moving some of it up to Sheffield eventually. A lot of staff chose to relocate there.

The building in Sussex Street no longer exists, having been demolished to make way for more housing.

Working at NU ended in 2003. The terrible incident at the Twin Towers, New York, and the sad loss of life meant Stock Markets worldwide were affected. Governments were jittery, and possible retaliations made the world unstable. The pensions we dealt with were invested in the markets. As they were defined contribution schemes, many people were worried, understandably, about their investments. The knock-on effect was that we had constant phone calls from concerned people, and sometimes there could be as many as fifty calls in an hour. This was hard, especially as we had to deal with the admin and paperwork side, too, and there were a lot of pressures.

This, coupled with pressures at home, I found too much. Though the company was there for me when I lost both my parents within four years, it affected me. My managers went out of their way to place me in teams with less work pressure, which helped me greatly. I spent a long time working with schemes which had become discontinued, and there were many of those too.

I decided I wanted to reduce my hours and try something different, so I left. My time there was good overall, and I made some good friends that I keep in touch with to this day. This, coupled with the many things I learnt, not least how to use a computer, have left me grateful for the experiences.

Final Employments 2003-2010 – A few months after leaving NU, I found part-time work in a B & B in Norwich for a while, but this was only temporary.

At this time, Vic and I were Homestay Hosts for teachers of English from different countries studying to improve their use of English in schools in their own countries. They were based and studying at NILE, which stands for *Norwich Institute for Language Education*. They studied there and attended lectures during the day but came home to stay with families. We were paid for looking after the teachers, but mainly it was in both sides' interest to spend time together in a home situation and share meals etc. We all enjoyed this time and benefited from each other's company, talking and learning about each other's ways of life. Over a few years on and off, we welcomed ladies from China. They stayed for longer than the others as it is far away, as well as Japan, Italy, Spain, France, Austria and Germany. They stayed for no more than a couple of weeks, but we only ever had two ladies stopping at a time. It was a enjoyable experience, and we all learnt a lot about each other's way of life. They became part of our family at the time.

In 2005, I secured a part-time position in Rymans the Stationers in Norwich at their shop inside the Castle Mall shopping area. It was strange that when I worked in Rose Lane in Norwich for NU many years before this, my colleagues and I had watched the Mall shopping area being built below the Castle from our Office windows, as the area had previously housed the old cattle market and auction area for many years since before the Wars. It was part of the regeneration of Norwich, and here I was working inside the Mall.

I worked there for five years and loved that too, as working part-time then suited me greatly. One of the stipulations of working there was that you had to work during the school holidays, especially during the long summer vacation, as the children are off and, of course, want to come in and get their new things for school. New pencil cases and pens were a great favourite.

It was good, and I loved working with my colleagues, who were a mixture of older ladies and young people – we had some good chats too. The main downside of the job was the tremendous heat, especially in the summer, as we had no air conditioning, only fans. The shop was inside and below ground in the Mall, and there were no windows. Some of the temperatures between 2003-2010 were over 30 degrees. I was glad I was only there for four hours a day as sometimes the hot atmosphere was truly faint-making, especially if the shop was busy, as it often was.

Looking back, my time there was good, but I decided to take early retirement in 2010.

Chapter Twenty-Six

My Favourite Film

I love many films, but one of my all-time favourites is *Jumping Jack Flash* with Whoopi Goldberg.

It came out in 1986 and is about a woman called Terry who works in a bank in America. Every day she goes to work doing the same old routine, logging in to the computer at her desk and starting her job.

Each day is the same until one day, she gets an unknown message on her screen from someone who asks for help. He says his name is Jack, and he is in trouble. What happens next is the film's theme. She becomes involved in a spy and espionage story, and her life takes a totally new turn.

It is a comedy but is very thrilling too. Until she gets the message on her computer, the only time there appears to be any excitement in the office is when sometimes her colleagues manage to get a link to a Russian TV channel by satellite. Then, they all stop work to watch the antics on the show. Of course, this was in the days before the World Wide Web that we have now, and it was not usual to see programmes from other countries on your computer, but as this film is a brilliant depiction of the 1980s, it works wonderfully. To see the clothes and hairstyles fashionable then is like stepping back in time, which is part of why I love this film.

You see, I had seen this film before I started my job at Norwich Union in 1989, and naturally, I thought my job would be like life in the bank in the film, but of course, without spies and adventures.

When I did commence there, it was like in the film at times, especially with the old-style computers and telephones with leads (no mobiles), fax machines and shredders that made up office life then. As well as the office banter and laughs, with colleagues, I had never experienced before.

When I watch this film again after all these years, it brings back those days, but with the adventure story that comes with it. One of the best bits in the film is when Whoopi gets her dress caught in the shredder as she tries to escape capture. Technology is different today in offices. You can have most of what you need in the palm of your hand.

This film impacted me so much that when I started work at NU, my first computer password was *JJFlash,* as I knew the memory of this film would help me remember it.

97

Chapter Twenty-Seven

Reflections from the Covid-19 Lockdown

I went to stay with my cousin Kris and her husband Roger on 13th March 2020. He was recovering from his hip operation. We hadn't seen them for about two years, and it had been planned for months.

Despite news about the Coronavirus in Wuhan in China becoming more widespread in Italy and Spain, being told constantly that it was spreading, and our eldest daughter telling me not to go to London, nothing was going to stop me.

So, I went armed with gloves for the touching of rails on the Underground as we had been told and had a lovely visit. We went to Kew Gardens on the Sunday to see the beautiful annual Orchid festival, and we were glad we did, as, within a few days, Kew was closed to the public.

News of the virus had begun to accelerate during the few days I was away, as had the virus, and it seemed to be getting worse in the UK.

I went with Kris one day to help her get stocked up with shopping as there was talk that the over seventies wouldn't be allowed out, which was the start of the panic buying. The shops were cleared of essentials, and there was no toilet roll to be found anywhere. People had started wearing masks, and life had suddenly become strange. I returned home on the 17th, which was eerie, as the train was almost empty.

I went to the hairdressers a few days later, and she said they had been busy as lots of people wanted to get their hair cut while they could. The news talked about a lockdown happening soon everywhere. The government gave daily announcements, and it was getting serious for us all. On the 23rd of March, our lockdown began.

To begin with, it was like living in a Sci-Fi film or the film *Outbreak* with Dustin Hoffman. There were queues at the shops for essential items, and the shelves were empty in many shops due to the panic buying by stupid people. I never thought I would have to queue on a high street outside a shop for essential toilet rolls for us and our immediate neighbours who are elderly. The towns had become like ghost towns, and that was weird.

We were getting daily bulletins from the government and *experts* giving figures to prove that many people were contracting the virus and then we were told about the daily deaths. It became too much, and we stopped watching the news. It still seemed to be happening in another world, and we were informed about it constantly. The worst thing, especially for those of us who were well, was being told we couldn't go out, losing personal freedom, and not being able to see friends and family. Vic's seventieth birthday was just before Easter, and we had to cancel all family celebrations, as did many other people.

We were told by the powers in charge, such as the World Health Organisation, that it was a worldwide pandemic and being in lockdown kept the rates of the virus down.

We have not been told the average death rates for each month of the year, so how can we know if the virus rates are worse than the usual mortality rate?

The world's economies are in free fall, and it will be a while before they improve. However, partly due to the media, many people are frightened and worrying unnecessarily. Did the government consider how people would have been affected in War times in the past? I don't think so. Of course, we live in a different world today, but still, it has been very sad.

Unlike many people, I have not panicked about the virus. Instead, I take each day as it comes and look forward to when it is all over, as that day will come. As Captain Tom, the 100-year-old war hero who has walked his garden and raised £30 million for the NHS, has reminded us.

There have been some positive parts of being in lockdown. Many of us have made this time a period of growth and a chance to catch up with tasks or things that never usually get done.

We have lived in Saltburn for six years, and this has been the first time we have had no visitors coming to see us. We haven't been anywhere other than our daily short walks, as permitted, so it has been a rest in some ways and a chance to re-group, as my brother-in-law states.

We have had more time to spend in our garden, which has been an escape from it all. Seeing it mature from the bare patch it was when we moved here to the plants emerging and growing from their long winter sleep has been a marvel. The sounds of nature, too, have inspired many people that would usually be too busy to hear them – like *our* blackbird who sings from the TV aerial daily.

For our eldest daughter and her family (our grandsons), it has been a period of re-growth. Their life is busy with their normal business, working from home, and homeschooling the boys. Still, they have turned much of their back garden into a small allotment and have started growing lots of vegetables. Despite not seeing them as we would have liked, we have face-timed them regularly, which has been a tonic to see them and catch up. They have enjoyed their time together and she is always positive.

As is always the case with our two daughters, the same cannot be said for our youngest. She has been alone in her accommodation in Bradford. She has managed somehow, as she always does, but with no TV, only a radio and a basic phone. Sometimes, I feel like she lives in a past life. Some days have been good for her, but many are bad, and when she is down and depressed, she calls us, and we get the tirade. We can do nothing more to help her situation as she must do it herself now, but it is still hard. When she is in full flow,

I come away shell-shocked but let her carry on as it may help her get matters off her chest. Hopefully, when the lockdown is lifted soon, we will be able to see her and try and counsel her further as I usually do. It helps when we have a lot of chats. She does well managing independently, but sometimes it is a trial for her, understandably.

This time has been bearable because of the knowledge our family and friends are sharing this with us. Thank goodness for modern technology and the ability to keep in touch with Whatsapp and Zoom. Especially when my sisters are far away in the States and on their own, a lot of the time, too, as our brothers-in-law are away. This has helped so much. Despite missing our activities and outings with friends in the U3A, we are now getting used to a new way of life.

Chapter Twenty-Eight

A Theatrical Moment

During the run-up to Christmas of 1979, we decided to take our eldest daughter, Stephanie, to the theatre in Norwich to see her first pantomime.

She had turned three in November, and we were living at 5 Woburn Street in Norwich then. Living in this house meant we were within walking distance of the Theatre Royal in the city centre.

We also had Rowan, who was born in July of that year and so, of course, was a baby. I think we must have had Vic's mum, Iris, over to babysit for her so we could go out. We probably went to the matinee and saw Cinderella at the theatre. The stars of the show were Yvonne Marsh as Prince Charming and Paul Henry as Buttons. Paul Henry was a well-known personality at that time for playing a character called Benny in Crossroads, a popular TV soap programme of the day. His trademark was to wear a woolly hat all the time, and he was portrayed as a comical character. Stephanie, of course, was too young to know of his popularity then. However, despite being her first time at theatre, she soon got into the spirit of Panto and the story of Cinderella and the Ugly Sisters and was amazed by all she saw. She sat between Vic and me, and we were in the middle, more or less, in the stalls, so we had a good view of the stage, and she could enjoy all the antics and performing that went on. When the Fairy Godmother appeared, it was magical, especially for a three-year-old. To see this lady in a beautiful white, sparkling dress waving her wand to change everything for Cinderella enthralled Stephanie.

During the second half of the show, the company did their set piece where they involved the audience more. It was billed in the programme as *Buttons and friends*. We didn't know what that meant, but we soon found out. Buttons appeared on the stage and asked if any children out there would like to come up and join him for some fun and games. A few older kiddies were eager, and off they went after being chosen by the characters in the production who picked them from the stage. Then one of the cast members came to the end of our row and asked our little girl if she would like to meet Buttons.

Stephanie was never shy as a small child, and after a bit of persuasion from us, she was led by the hand and followed the young actress to the stage.

By the time she got there, Buttons was in line with about eight children of varying ages and heights. Stephanie was led to the end of the row and was the smallest. Then, of course, there were the inevitable *ahhs* from the audience, and she looked a picture on the stage. Vic and I were very proud and choked with emotion to see our little girl on the stage of the Theatre Royal.

Then Buttons started his game. He interviewed all the children one by one, and when he got to Stephanie, he had to go down on his knees as she was tiny compared to the others. A few laughs ensued, and lots of clapping followed from the audience. Next, buttons sang with the children.

When it was finished, an assistant gave the other children a small gift and some sweets or something. Then they all departed from the stage to rejoin their respective families.

Eventually, all that was left was Paul Henry in his bobble hat, dressed in the traditional costume of Buttons, and our little girl on the stage. Being so young, she looked even smaller in the big auditorium. Then after the last child had departed, Buttons made out it was all over, and he was on his own. He stood quite a way

103

away from her. Stephanie just stood there looking alone and forlorn, and there were again many *ahhs* from the audience.

Surprisingly, she didn't cry as many children may have done, being left to stand there alone for a short while until, eventually, Buttons came over and spoke to her. After that, I think she had to sing, but when the interview was over, he told her he had a special surprise. She was told to close and cover her eyes, which she did, and just then, the Fairy Godmother came on stage with her wand, and when Stephanie saw her, she was amazed. We were over the moon, and then the Fairy Godmother produced a huge bag of gifts and toys for our lucky little girl to take home. Stephanie said, 'Thank you,' very audibly on stage, and there was a lot of clapping from the audience. She was truly thrilled and stunned by it all, and when she came back to join us in the stalls, there was a lot of chatting and hugging, as you can imagine, about our daughter's *Theatrical Moment*.

Chapter Twenty-Nine

A Blast from The Past

A few years ago, since we moved up here to Saltburn-by-the-Sea, we took a trip back to places we remembered that were important to us. This would have been about 2017 and was during a visit to Norwich and Norfolk when we went to see our family.

East Rudham – To begin with, we went to the village of East Rudham, which is in North Norfolk. This is where Vic – my husband – grew up and lived during his formative years.

After Iris, my dear mother-in-law, died in 2015, the family arranged to have a bench made and erected on the village green with a lovely plaque. This was to remember both his parents, who were born and lived much of their lives there. They had many happy memories of times in the village. Vic's grandmother, his nanna, also called Vicki Makins, is remembered in the cemetery there, along with his grandfather. The village has fond memories for me, too, as Vic and I spent the first six months of our married life in 1975 living there with Nanna until we moved to Norwich.

West Raynham – After spending about an hour in the village, we decided to go to the camp of West Raynham, which is no more than three miles away.

Many RAF camps were built in East Anglia during the Second World War. Some are near each other due to the proximity across the Wash to Germany.

My dad was posted and worked at West Raynham for many years, and it was at the camp's *Kestrel club* where Vic and I first met in late 1973. So, we thought we'd go along to see how the camp had changed, as now it is no longer *operational*, to quote a RAF term.

The last time we visited there was in 2005 when we took Vic's parents out for a ride on their 50th Wedding Anniversary. We were genuinely shocked when we saw how most of the camp had become dilapidated and overgrown with long grass and weeds everywhere. It is a fact that when the Services leave a place after it is no longer needed, the camps that were once teeming with life become like ghost towns, and it is quite strange and eerie. Seeing sheep feeding on the grass growing outside what had once been the Kestrel Club and the NAAFI, where we once frequented, was very sad.

This time, we were pleasantly surprised to see and discover that a big notice outside the entrance to the former RAF base stated that the camp was being redeveloped as a private concern. All the former houses built and owned by the RAF have been sold at peppercorn prices, and now people are living in them. It is still overgrown and tatty in parts, but at least it looked tidier and more welcoming for new people to live in.

For me, though, the best part of this visit was when I saw the fenced-off area near the former entrance to the camp where the RAF plane used to be, as they are in many RAF bases. There was a big notice and a pyramid sort of erection plinth. This has been put as a tribute and memorial to those who worked and served at this former base.

I have attached a photo which show the memorial. It details the Kestrel squadron, a joint operation between the British, (West) German and American forces beginning in 1964. This was what my dad was involved with, as he worked on these planes in his role as an Airframe fitter, and therefore we came as a family to Norfolk. The Kestrel aeroplane was the forerunner of what later became the Harrier Jump Jet in this joint venture with the other countries.

Memorial to all who were stationed and worked at RAF West Raynham

I was choked and humbled when I read the inscriptions on the pyramid, as it made me prouder of my dad and all the work he was involved in. It is a truly fitting memorial, and I hope one day his descendants, starting with his grandchildren and great-grandchildren, will get to see it. As a postscript to this, West Raynham and surrounding areas of the local countryside were used in the 60s to film *Operation Crossbow*, a film set in the Second World War. My dad was there when this was filmed.

Syderstone – We went a little further on until we came to the village of Syderstone. This is where two of my sisters and I attended the village primary school for a few years during the middle 1960s when we lived at RAF Sculthorpe, which is sited about two miles from there.

When Vic and I decided to get married, it was at the church in Syderstone. This is the nearest parish church to the camp. It is known as St Mary's in Syderstone. Its claim to fame is that outside there is a big notice board that states, *Amy Robsart once worshipped here*. In the 1500s, she was the wife of the Earl of Essex, Robert Dudley. He was a favourite and, supposedly, a lover of Queen Elizabeth I. History shows that Amy Robsart later died by falling, or she was pushed, down the stairs of their ancestral home. So, the story goes.

However, it is a big and typical Norman church, and this is where we were married in 1975.

We were looking around outside and reminiscing when this lady came out and asked if we wanted to go in. They had just finished

the Sunday service and were having coffee. So, we accepted and joined them, telling the churchgoers that we were just looking around as we had been married there years before. They thought it was great and wanted us to sign their visitor's book, especially as it has been a number of years since we had been back there. So, we duly did, and I asked a lady if someone would mind taking our photo at the church door. She asked a man if he would take a picture of this *young couple,* as she put it. That made our day as we had already been married over forty years.

Sculthorpe, formerly RAF Sculthorpe – After leaving Syderstone and the church that day, we made our way back to Norwich by way of passing the village towards what had once been Sculthorpe camp – my home for a few years in my middle to late teens. I lived in a bungalow on what was once 701a Coventry Street – this was where I got married from, and our wedding reception was held there. My mum and mother-in-law made and prepared this. We had a party where all my relations living in Essex, which was quite a number, Vic's family, and our friends all came and celebrated with us. This was a lot of people to have in that bungalow, but we managed somehow.

The bungalows are all at the end of the camp, away from the brick-built RAF houses on another part of the base. These bungalows are affectionately known as *tobacco houses.* Built for the Americans in the USAF Tactical Fighter Wing and their families stationed there during the Second World War and many years afterwards. Probably until the 1980/90s, when the USAF left, and the bungalows were sold to private buyers again at peppercorn prices.

They were called tobacco houses as the British had them built for the Americans serving during the War, but they were paid for by the American Government, giving tobacco, cigarettes and cigars to the British troops who were serving in the War. Smoking was looked on differently in those days, as it was seen as helping troops in their stress in the fight for freedom.

As quite a few years had passed since we returned to Sculthorpe, we were surprised to see the former camp had been renamed *Wicken Green,* presumably after the farmer whose land it once was. We could enter where the camp gate once stood, and we took a short ride around to wallow in the nostalgia. It was strange to see it all again. Even more so when I realised the bungalows had hardly changed apart from personal changes made by the new owners such as doors, windows and gardens. Considering the bungalows had only been meant to last for the duration of the war years, they have done well to be still there and lived in after more than seventy years. The streets have all been renamed too, and when we found what was once Coventry Street is now Rose Avenue – I think – it brought back many memories. A former life for us both.

What I did find odd, though, was when we drove to where the former airfield once was – which had the longest heated runway in Europe, incidentally – I was taken aback to see that many of the old buildings remained. Very old and dilapidated, but the single men's barrack blocks were there, along with the gymnasium and other buildings. It was here where the former NCOs club used to be. Vic and I had been many a time to dances on Saturday night, in the most popular club in Norfolk during the 1970s, as it was known. The Vietnam war was on during my time there, and many of the people

we knew from that period had been there.
So, all in all, we had really been on a *blast from the past.*

Chapter Thirty

Animals I Have Known

Growing up in the RAF meant my three sisters and I moved around a bit, so, despite our numerous requests for a pet, especially a dog, we were not allowed to have one. This was because, in Dad's words, 'It wouldn't be fair on the dog', which now I can see.

Going abroad and being moved to various parts of the UK would have entailed quarantine as well as the upheaval and the costs, of course, which I know our parents wouldn't have been able to afford.

Our pleas went unheeded until we had our first pet for a little while as Dad finally relented, and one day he got us a dog. It was a Basset Hound puppy whom we named Ben after the Michael Jackson song of the same name – I think. This was about 1969-70 when that song came out. We all loved and petted him, of course, but needless to say, having no experience with pets, my sisters and I were loath to take him out regularly. So, the inevitable task fell on Dad most of the time, and as our mum had a part-time job in a grocery store on the camp then, and Dad worked long hours, it was all a bit much for them, I know.

I'm sorry to say the dog had to go after about three months and was sold, which we were all sorry for, but we obviously didn't appreciate then that a dog, especially a puppy, must be house trained and walked. All we wanted was to have Ben sitting on our laps and being stroked.

We were all sad for a while, but it was perhaps fate as shortly after that, Dad was posted to Germany, where we moved to for three years.

So, that was the end of a family pet when I was young. It was not until years later, when my sisters and I were all married and had our own families, that we had some pets.

In my own family, after much discussion, Vic and I again decided against getting a dog as the responsibility is great, and we had a busy life with a young family. We started with a few fish in a tank and then moved on to a succession of hamsters and guinea pigs, not all at the same time. We got these for our daughters Stephanie and Rowan when they were about six to ten. They loved them, and I'm pleased to say they looked after them. The girls were happy to clean their hutches and wash up the hamster equipment with Vic's help.

Vic had been brought up with animals, living in the countryside. They had dogs in his family when he was young, so he was more used to animal welfare. Our girls loved their small animals, and we had a lot of fun and good times watching them play in their runs or the house.

One time, the hamster *Hammy* escaped from his cage when the door was not shut properly, and we couldn't find him anywhere. He disappeared for about three days, and we thought that was the end of him. Then one early evening, we heard these noises coming from behind the fireplace where we still had the chimney, which housed the gas fire. Then all of a sudden, he appeared! It seems he had been in the chimney breast and looked none the worse for it, despite having a couple of singed whiskers from when the fire had been on and he was behind it. Just as well it was a gas fire. It was a relief to see him, and the girls were happy too.

Then we had Tweetie Pie. He was mine, a lovely green and yellow budgie Vic bought me to keep me company when the girls were at school as I didn't work then. We had a white one for a while whom we called *Snowy*, and they were company for each other in the same cage. Until one day, this bird was flying around the room – we used to let them do this now and again – and unfortunately got out of a small open window. Despite looking for her, we never saw her again.

I spent a lot of time talking to Tweetie Pie and trying to get him to talk. We had heard that if you get birds, mostly the males when they are young, they can be taught to speak. So, I spent many times at the cage door saying, 'Hello, Tweetie Pie,' all to no avail.

Then after a couple of years and totally out of the blue, I heard this shrill voice saying, 'Hello, Tweetie Pie,' and he started to repeat this many times. We listened to this over and over from him, and it was lovely to hear. This was followed by a voice saying, 'Come here, Stephanie,' many times. He had obviously heard me saying it and could mimic my voice perfectly. We were amazed to hear our bird say this, and I was pleased and proud that he had started to talk. After that, we often heard him talking to himself and chirping away as I got on with my chores.

Then one Saturday morning, we were all clearing up as a family around the house, and Vic was doing the vacuuming. To save time, he decided to do the bottom of the budgie cage, which was always covered in seed bits and droppings, so he stuck the nozzle in the door. The next thing, poor Tweetie, was up the pipe. What a fright!

He quickly removed the nozzle and pipes and managed to rescue the budgie by blowing in the pipe. Of course, he was covered in dust and must have been scared, but at least he was alive.

Vic was in the doghouse for a while, and we looked after Tweetie after that experience, but I don't think he ever really recovered as a couple of months after that, I woke up one morning to find him dead on the floor of his cage. We, mostly me, were distraught to lose him, and I shall never forget how he learned to talk. He was buried in the garden of that old house in Woburn Street, along with the other guineas and hamsters we lost over time. I once wrote to the local newspaper about him when they wanted pet stories.

Part II

After our brief period of having a dog when we were young, my three sisters and I have since all become dog owners. Having dogs has quite literally changed our lives.

As my sister Debra has told me with the fridge magnet she bought me stating, *Dogs are not our whole life, but they make our lives whole.*

My sister's dogs in the USA.

Debra and her family have had the most dogs over the years of various breeds. She lost her Golden Retriever, Cadbury, after many years – he lived till nearly twelve – and now has two smaller dogs, Winston and Sadie.

I have never met them, but I am often sent photos and see them regularly during our contact by WhatsApp and Email. We, of course, don't see each other much, as Debra, like all my sisters, lives in the States. She lives in Georgia now.

Debra's twin Lee lives in Texas, near the coast in Corpus Christi. Lee and her family had their dog, Rascal, an American Cocker Spaniel, for a long time until, unfortunately, she suddenly lost him about eighteen months ago. He was nearly thirteen when he died, and she is still too upset to get another dog but says she will one day. But, again, I only ever saw photos of him, and when she showed me how he was settled on the settee during a call – he looked like a lovely dog.

Kerry, my youngest sister, had two Great Danes quite a few years ago. She had one, a dog, and then acquired another, a white bitch they called *Snowy*. One of her neighbours on the base where she was living at the time was moving abroad and couldn't take the dog, so Kerry and her family had the dog and had both of them for a long time, though great Danes don't live long due to their size.

When we visited Kerry in 2002, we met the Great Danes. They were lovely dogs and truly gentle giants. They wouldn't hurt you, but they slobbered all over you, which was a mess.

Kerry lived in Arizona then, and of course, it is very hot, being in a desert. It gets to 110deg F, sometimes higher in the summer, and she told me how hot it is to walk the dogs as the pavements are burning. She said they could really do with shoes. When we returned to England, I made some shoes for them out of pieces of material with leather elbow patches sewn in as the soles of the feet. I attached pieces of strong laces through the tops to pull together around the dog's ankles, so to speak, and this worked. I sent them to Kerry, and she said they worked a treat, making it much more comfortable for the dogs to walk outside.

Bandit

Eventually, after a lot of years, we were able to get a dog.

We got our dog *Bandit* in 2006 when he was seven weeks old. We bought him from a reputable breeder in a place called Hingham, just a few miles outside Norwich. This town's claim to fame, by the way, is that it is the birthplace of Abraham Lincoln's family before they emigrated to the States, and from a historical point of view, there is a memorial to this as well as a big piece in the church about the Lincoln family. However, we visited the breeder and saw where Bandit came from. He is a Lhasa Apso cross with a Bichon Frise, his mother being the Lhasa and his dad the Bichon. He was the smallest in the litter and came to us immediately, and that was that. He is called Bandit because he has a mask over his eyes – a black and white mixture dog.

We brought him home, and he has been part of our family ever since, now almost fifteen years old. Like all dogs, he has a definite personality of his own and a confident attitude which Lhasas are famous for. He is loving but stubborn, and if he doesn't want to do something, he won't and literally digs his feet in. However, he is as

115

cheeky as he always was and is quite a character.

I always said we would *have dog will travel*, and he has been everywhere we have been – on buses, in the car and on trains, as well as the odd boat. He has been to many places around the country, and there are not many places he hasn't *weed* on – Canterbury Cathedral, Hastings, Hadrian's Wall, Ripon, York, the Lake District, and Norwich, to name but a few and up Roseberry Topping when we went a few years ago, and I have written about in a previous story.

We gave up holidays abroad when we got him, and he always comes on holiday with us, to a caravan or a cottage. It is especially wonderful since we moved to Saltburn a few years ago. He loves the beach, too, along with many of the little doggie friends he has made.

He is becoming more human as he gets older. Especially as he has spent much more time with us in the last couple of years during the lockdown periods of the Coronavirus pandemic. He is definitely part of the family.

Chapter Thirty-One

A Stroll Around the Garden

When I was young and growing up on RAF camps, my family didn't have much interest in gardening. In fact, it would not be an understatement to say my dad hated it, and the only thing he ever did was to cut the grass and then only when he had to.

Mum did take a little more interest and grew a few flowers once. Still, she never really had the time with the four of us to bring up, and life was busy. It was inevitable that one day we would leave the RAF house and move somewhere else, and any growing and hard work in the garden would be left for the following families.

Not everyone was like Dad. Some people did have beautiful gardens, and it must have been a wrench for them when they had to leave that house and garden.

Moving is a way of life in the Services.

When I met Vic in 1974, and we married the following year, I saw gardening from a different perspective. His family were from the country and actually lived in the next village to where we lived on the RAF camp – Sculthorpe in Norfolk. (Though I didn't know that at the time).

His parents, my in-laws, Stanley and Iris, were avid gardeners

117

and, years before I knew them had an allotment where all things were grown.

As the years went by and they moved to two different houses in Dereham, their gardens were lovely. Then when Stanley had his major stroke in 1989, and life changed for both of them, the garden for Iris became her escape and sanctuary.

When we visited them in their bungalow, the flowers and plants she grew were a picture, and she had an incredible display of pots in the summer too. That is one of the things I remember with much sadness, too, because when she got dementia in her later years, the garden went to pot, and she gave up caring for it. One of the downsides of the illness was she couldn't remember what to do. Very sad, but I think seeing what Iris did before then must have nurtured the seeds in me to take an interest in gardening.

In my married life, in the two houses we had in Norwich, Vic did all the gardening, I took care of the house, and both of us brought up our family.

Our gardens went from nothing when we moved there to some flowers and maturity over the years. I do remember we planted a Victoria plum tree at the back of 5 Woburn Street, our first house. It grew to quite a size in the fourteen years we lived there. It was lovely to see the blossoms in spring and the fruit.

Then at Blakeney Close, we planted a Stella cherry tree out front that matured into a lovely tree during the twenty-three years we lived there. It gave us shade for the front of the house and the blossom and cherries of the seasons.

Leaving those gardens and the house we lived in then was a wrench, but they say a house is built of bricks and mortar and made by the family that dwelt there, and it was our time to move on. So, we came here to Saltburn in 2014 to our Park Home at Hazel Grove Residential park.

When we initially came here in 2013, there was nothing but a plot for us to choose where our home was to be sited. We brought one or two plants from our old garden in Norwich with us. A chrysanthemum and a Fatsia Japonica and planted them in the garden. The chrysanthemum blooms with beautiful maroon-red flowers in November, my birthday month. The Fatsia Japonica has grown from a small shrub and is now huge in the back garden and very bushy. It seems to like the heavy clay soil found here in the north. Despite being such heavy soil and difficult to work with at times, it still amazes me the amount and range of beautiful flowers growing here. All our work in our garden has been worth it as we have turned our new plot area into quite a lovely garden with plants and flowers of many types.

I am particularly proud of the Peonies that have only come out in the last couple of years and are a beautiful crimson pink. I planted them about five years ago with a few bulbs/corms I bought from a Poundland store, and I thought they were dead. Then, suddenly, they bloomed two years ago and are now blooming again – to my pride and joy.

I have developed green fingers as most of the things I have planted have grown and thrived. Maybe I have more time now, but I love being out in the garden, and along with Vic's help, we have much pleasure in planting seeds and watching them grow.

We have planted another cherry tree out in the front too. This one is a Morello and is suitable for eating if the birds leave it alone.

The lockdown periods of last year, 2020, and then again in recent months have been a godsend to us. We have spent many happy hours in our garden and planted many different types of plants. My current favourite is Hellebores – I love the flowers.

When out in the garden with the blackbirds singing along with other birds, what more could you wish for? How I love my garden view.

If you have a garden and a library, you have everything you need.

by Cicero (BC)

Chapter Thirty-Two

A Great Time Together

On Saturday 20th August 2021, our family from Norwich came here to see us. Stephanie, our eldest daughter, with Andrew, her partner, and our two grandsons, Jasper and Freddie.

We hadn't seen each other for over a year due to the coronavirus pandemic of the last eighteen months, and with everyone around the country being kept in by the various lockdowns forced onto us by the powers that be. It was with much excitement that we awaited their arrival. The last time they were here, they stayed in a cottage in Loftus, not far from here, and they did this again as they need their own space just as we do here. Me, Vic and Bandit are used to being on our own for most of the time here in Saltburn.

They travelled up on the Friday and came to see us early on Saturday morning. Needless to say, it was raining when they arrived and plans to go out were not to be. However, as we hadn't seen each other for so long, we had lots to catch up on. They had already had three days in the Derbyshire Peak District in a cottage before arriving here and were glad of a rest.

We opened the front door to them, and they all trooped in one by one. First Stephanie, then Freddie, followed by Jasper and finally Andrew.

Each one was greeted with a hug and kiss to make up for lost time. It was wonderful, with plenty of comments about how the boys had grown. Jasper is thirteen now and a little taller than me, so we were amazed, and Freddie is nine and almost as tall.

We all settled down with cups of coffee and biscuits and chatted. First, they told us about their time in Derbyshire, near Matlock, and when they visited Eyam, known as the plague village. It was particularly poignant to go there this year so the boys could see plague and lockdowns were not new. In the 1600s, the village of Eyam had the plague brought to them by fleas found in bolts of cloth, which a travelling salesman/merchant brought from London. Many people and whole families lost their lives, as seen in the churchyard and the graves.

This was quite a sad but real part of their trip, but they made up for it the next day by going to the *Heights of Abraham*, a big amusement park with lots of adventure rides. They showed me photos of them up in cable cars above the trees. I'm glad I wasn't there with them, not liking heights.

After lunch, we played a *Harry Potter Scrabble* from a set I had bought earlier in the year when Aldi had a Harry Potter day of things for sale. I saved this set for when they came.

Jasper and Freddie teamed up, and we had a lot of fun along with a few laughs at some of the words they came out with, trying to fool us with words they had made up but said they were from the magic world.

By the time we finished playing, the weather had improved, and we decided to go for a little walk.

We had recently bought a pushchair for Bandit as he has been having trouble with his legs due to his age and probably arthritis. Freddie wanted to push him some of the way, which he did.

We walked around Saltburn and to the sweetshop, which they entered with gusto and had lots of sweets. This was a special treat for the boys, and from there, we went down the bank, which was no joke with the pushchair, to reach the amusement arcades on the pier where lots of money was spent too. They love the arcade, like all children on wet days at the seaside. My purse, of course, was lighter too, giving them money.

After a couple of hours, we returned home and had fish and chips for supper. We had a lovely day, and it was a good start to the rest of the week with them.

Sunday 22nd August – On Sunday, we went to Raby Castle, near Bishop Auckland – one of the oldest castles in the country – for the day. This was the former home of the Neville family that Richard III became part of when he married into them in the 1400s. We didn't go into it as dogs are not allowed, but we walked around the extensive grounds and the two lakes. The gardens are beautiful and well maintained, with lots of lovely late summer flowers in bloom. There was a puzzle trail where the children had to find secret plaques from fairy stories in the gardens and mark them off on a sheet which the boys enjoyed doing.

We took Bandit in the pushchair as it was a lot for him and entirely uphill in parts too. The weather wasn't brilliant, but we had a nice day out together, had a picnic outside, and went to the café that catered for dogs.

Monday 23rd August – Our family went for a walk from Robin Hood's Bay along the cliff top. Stephanie said it was for about six miles and quite arduous – I am glad we stayed home to rest. They naturally were quite tired and returned to their cottage after a short visit to us.

Tuesday 24th August – At last, the boys had their beach day on Tuesday. The weather had picked up a bit by then and was good for swimming in the sea.

They had new body boards and were like professional surfers, loving every minute. Their mum and dad were in with them too and having lots of fun as a family. They are all active and keep fit, which is good. Vic and I stayed with the beach stuff and enjoyed our day doing very little.

Wednesday 25th August – The next day we went out together for a walk on the Moors. After a drive across them, which were out in lots of heather, we came to Egton Bridge and parked the cars next to St Hedda's Church in an old coal yard which has been there for years. Then, after going a little way up the road and past the church, we turned left onto a track between the trees, which leads to Grosmont. This was the old toll road, and a sign is up on an old house, part way there, which tells you how much the tolls were to go here in 1948. The road is about two miles long but is all flat, and we took Bandit with us in the pushchair again.

We had a lovely walk and chatted together as we were going along. The scenery on either side is spectacular too, and there are lots to look at. Then we reached Grosmont and stopped at the picnic benches outside the station to have our packed lunches. Jasper was fighting off a wasp, as is the norm in August when you are eating outside.

After we looked around the station platforms and the shops, I bought the boys an ice cream. It was lovely to see the steam trains going in and out of the station and waving to all the passengers. There were a lot of people there too.

Despite walking back again on the toll road to the cars at Egton Bridge, it was a good day. We went home tired but happy.

Thursday 26th August – Thursday was their last day with us, and we had a quiet day at home, resting a little, and playing Harry Potter Scrabble again, which was a lot of fun.

After a quick lunch I had prepared earlier in the morning, we had to go to the beach again. Freddie was desperate to go in the sea one more time. Despite the weather being cold and with a freezing wind, it was good for flying their kite on the beach. We stayed with Stephanie and Jasper on the sand whilst Andrew had to go into the sea with Fred to play in the surf. The sea did have big surf waves then, and it was admirable of his dad to go in and look after him. The beach lifeguards were standing by as there were a few people in the sea despite the cold. They weren't in too long and came back to get dried and warm.

After this, one more trip to the amusement arcades on the pier was required until Vic and I left to go home as we had left Bandit there. They all packed and went back to their cottage to get changed, rest a little, and do a little packing for their return the next day.

We had arranged to meet later for an evening meal at the *Longacre* at Skelton. We had a great time and a good meal discussing our adventures.

After this, sadly, we had to say goodbye for the time being, as they had to leave early the next day from the cottage.

After a long journey home, they are back in Norwich to work and prepare for the boy's return to their schools and a new term.

After a strange couple of years in lockdown, at least we had some time together and have wonderful memories of our holiday together.

Chapter Thirty-Three

A Monetary Matter

Many years ago, in a previous life, when my sisters and I were small, our parents taught and encouraged us to play lots of games. Not only board games such as Ludo and Monopoly but various card games.

Our mum and dad had always been avid card players, especially at Whist. For many years they went to Whist Drives and won many prizes. They enjoyed it, and it gave them a social outlet, too, as sometimes they played in teams such as Partner Whist. I expect they just wanted to pass on the fun and games they had to us. There is a saying, *A family that plays together stays together*.

In the 1960s, when we lived in Norfolk, at 6 Woq house, Tattersett (outside RAF Sculthorpe), we often used to have our relatives from Essex stay with us and visit in the holidays.

One of these was Uncle Ron, my dad's brother, who was a bit of a gambler on the quiet. He taught us, and we had a lot of fun playing games with him, like *gin rummy* and *pontoon* and *chase the ace*. Other times, our Auntie Kit, one of Mum's sisters, and Uncle Don came to stay, and we spent many happy hours playing games with them. I remember, particularly after we had gone to bed, that they used to sit up until late in the evening playing card games with Mum and Dad. They were enjoyable times.

One card game we were taught to play was *Newmarket,* and we often played this with Mum and Auntie Kit. These are the rules:

You lay out the four Kings from the pack on the table, and then the dealer gives out all the cards to the players, plus two sets of hands to himself. The dealer then picks one set and leaves the other one closed on the table away from the game being played, which is not used.

When we were younger, we were given counters to put on the Kings, but as we got older, we were encouraged to put pennies or halfpennies – as they were around then – on the cards, the currency being pounds shillings and pence. Mum used to tell us it would teach us the value of money and how to accept losing, which I suppose it did. It also helped my youngest sister with her sums.

The players put one coin on a King and another in the middle, which became the *Kitty* or winnings. The final object was to get rid of all your cards to win the kitty.

The game starts with the dealer, and a card is laid from the hands you have. Each player then must follow suit with consecutive cards of the same suit that followed the one the first player laid. Cards are laid in order from your own hand if you have them. For example, ace being 1, then 2,3,4,5, etc. – ending with the Queen, which means if you do have the Queen, you then become the winner of that suit by taking away any money that may be on the King of the same. The suits were played in alternate colours of red and black. You then carry on with the game until winnings are found on the relevant King to the Queen you may have in your hand, and when all cards are used, the kitty is won too.

For many happy hours, we played this game, and it passed away many wet days.

We played for a long time on this particular day until the money had built up onto one specific King. Then, the Kings are gradually taken from the table to shorten the game. For example, you would be unlucky if you have the Queen of Diamonds in your hand and that King is removed from the table. You would not obviously get any money that would have been placed on it. There were many sighs of *Ohhh,* if that happened.

However, on this day, only one King was left, and the money built up on it repeatedly, until first there were brown coins of pennies and halfpennies, then sixpences and shillings – a five pence – and then a florin – in today's money two shillings equals ten pence. This was a lot of money to us when we were about eleven years old like me and nine years old as my sisters were. We didn't

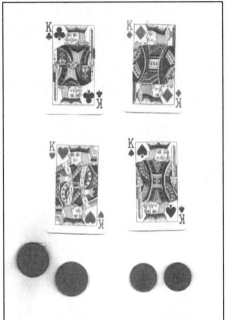

have much in those days so this amount would probably have bought about a year's worth of sweets.

The money went up again as finally, half a crown – worth two shillings and sixpence – was laid on the King to replace the substantial pile of coins that had built up. Then a silver florin was laid along with the silver-coloured half a crown, totalling four shillings and sixpence. In today's money, that amount would probably be about £20.

As children, our eyes were out like organ stops looking at this and wishing we could win it. Finally, the dealer, who I think was my mum, dealt the hands for the final time, and when I looked at my hand, I had the Queen that belonged to the King with all the money on it. Years of playing has taught me to be stoical or have a poker face, as they say. I kept it quiet, and we started to play.

We all took turns playing one card down at a time, starting with the lowest black card – the ace representing a one. That means the lowest black card to be laid by the person next to the dealer. Then, around the table, we followed with the consecutive cards that followed the card which had been placed before. If black cards ran out, you moved on to the red ones. Eventually, most of the cards in our hands were gone until we came to the ten, Jack and Queen, which were the same suit as the King with all the money placed onto it – the two silver coins I mentioned.

I can't recall which suit the King was, but I know it was a red one. I laid the Queen we were all waiting for. An eruption occurred from all the players as I had won the money on the King! Then as it was my last card, the money in the kitty was mine too.

That was the end of that game of Newmarket and the fun of the game too. Despite playing numerous times over the years, we have never experienced a game with so much tension and excitement as that one. Even now, many years later, my sisters and I still talk about the day I won all the money. Much to their annoyance.

Chapter Thirty-Four

A Memorable Gift

In the early 1970s, I lived in Germany with my parents and sisters. Dad was posted to RAF Laarbruch, close to the Dutch border. The Dutch city of Nijmegen (a town of much conflict during the Second World War) and the town of Venlo were relatively close by.

However, we lived just a few miles from the RAF camp in a small German town called Weeze.

Due to the high numbers of service personnel and their families, there wasn't enough accommodation at the camp for all. The RAF had presumably leased housing in the nearest towns of Weeze and Goch, and a shuttle bus used to run between them to the camp and back. We lived in a third-floor flat in new blocks of flats in Weeze. As we were outside the camp, most of our essential shopping was done in the town's local areas within walking distance.

As well as a little grocery store and the Sparkasse bank nearby, another shop I remember well was the jewellers. Being all girls in our family, we naturally found this shop interesting and often looked around it. When I was seventeen, I had my ears pierced in the shop by this jeweller, and my sisters awaited their turn when the time came.

However, for my sixteenth birthday, which was in 1971, Mum

and Dad bought me a silver bracelet from that jeweller in Weeze. I honestly can't remember if I had seen it first and admired it or if Mum got it as a surprise, but it certainly became the start of a special present.

The bracelet had a Pfennig coin dipped in silver on it. This was before the Euro came into EU countries, and the currency was Marks and Pfennigs.

I was thrilled with this bracelet and wore it all the time. Then, when I had a little money to spare from my savings, I bought a couple more charms from the jeweller to be put on the bracelet. In addition, I got a shield of the town of Goch and other nearby towns.

After Dad's tour ended, we returned to the UK in late 1973, and in due course, I applied to and attended King's Lynn College of Arts & Technology, where I took my A levels. (I have written about this elsewhere).

I spent over two years living and studying in King's Lynn, and the town became familiar to me. I found a silver charm in a shop there one day. It was the town's coat of arms, having once been very important in history. I had to buy this and had the local jeweller add it to my bracelet. Collecting things had always been part of my nature, and this became the start of adding charms to my bracelet.

During this time, I met Vic, and we eventually married in 1975. He, of course, was happy to help me add charms too. He often went with me to the various shops we had looked for whilst visiting places on holiday.

When our daughters came along, it became a common thing for them to get me a charm for my birthday or Christmas, with their dad's help, of course. We remember to this day how much searching was done in all the various towns we were visiting to find a named charm for me.

On that first bracelet, I added shields or coat of arms of London, Tintagel in Cornwall, Glastonbury, Cornwall, Newquay, Ilfracombe (Devon), Matlock, Shanklin and the Isle of Wight, as well as Norwich and Miami, Florida. These all represent memorable times and holidays I had with my family, especially as this was when my girls were little. I look back on those times now gone with many fond memories.

Over time, the bracelet got rather full, and when I went out to work, I thought it might be nice to have another so I would have one to leave to each of my two daughters when I am gone. Vic bought me another one when we lived in Norwich, much later in the 1980s, for my Christmas present one year. This one has a model of a Scorpion on it, this being my birth sign and the emblem of Norfolk's coat of arms. It began another period of getting charms from places we visited and added to this bracelet. There are charms from York, Wales, Woburn Abbey and Portsmouth to name a few. All places we visited as a family.

There is one shield on this one I didn't visit, which is of a place called Gruyeres, in Switzerland. This is from a holiday Stephanie and Rowan went on with the Girl Guides when they were of middle school-age. Their first time away from home to another country. Needless to say, they had a whale of a time, and I treasure this charm as they bought it themselves and brought it back for me.

These days, I don't wear my bracelets much anymore, but when I look at them, they are truly a wonderful memory of times gone by.

Chapter Thirty-Five

A Brush with Crime

Iwas a bit of a rebel in my early to middle teens. I'm unsure whether this was due to my age, my hormones, the changing times we lived in during the 1960s and 70s, or a mixture. However, I know that Bob Dylan, the singer/poet of the time, had it all right when he made his famous anthem of the time, *The times they are a' changing.*

We moved to Germany in 1970, and my sisters and I were sent to boarding school – the only option, as there was no secondary school on the camp we lived in. This was in the days of the British Services of the Rhine. There were quite a few dependent children of Army and RAF personnel who went to various boarding schools across, what was then, West Germany.

We went to Windsor Girls' School in a town called Hamm, which is in North Rhine Westphalia, and we were there for three years, coming home at the end of terms for the school holidays. Our times there were good overall and certainly an experience. We were looked after well by the teaching and admin staff.

We were kept busy all the time, and our days were run by a series of bells and timetables, with little free time. Thinking back, it was quite strict, but it couldn't be anything else with over a thousand girls aged eleven to eighteen.

However, this meant, at certain times, lack of freedom became a bit much, and now and again, we *got up to no good*, as my mother used to say.

I remember when the other girls and I hatched a plan to raid the kitchens, which we did a few times. It wasn't as though we were hungry as we were fed well with five good meals and snacks every day, but I suppose it was boredom, the strict routines and being away from home that led us to *wanting an adventure* as the novels of the time said. So, we got together and planned to go to the dining room after lights out.

Thinking back, it was daring, and if we had been caught, we would've been in serious trouble and maybe even expelled. That didn't worry us at the time, though.

About four or five of us dressed in black clothes sneaked out of the house, about five blocks away from the dining room. Then we went into the dining room, which wasn't locked, and through into the back kitchens where we filled our bags with biscuits, cakes and anything else we could hide. Then, being as quiet as possible, we ran back to our house and quickly went back to bed.

The next night meant we had a midnight feast in our dorms. Of course, all the girls were sworn to secrecy, and as I have said, we were lucky to get away with it, not considering it a crime at the time. It was just a big adventure as we saw it.

Nobody seemed to have noticed anything was missing from the store cupboards, at least we weren't told by staff, so I guess they may have known it was the girls. I don't know. We were just lucky to not have been caught.

However, the next incident that girls from my house were involved with was another matter. Every end of term at Windsor, each year group had a *Social,* as it was known, a get-together with the boys from the neighbouring Windsor Boys' School. It was a big event with music, and all the girls looked forward to their dance and a chance to dress up.

On this occasion, it was the end of the Christmas term – 1971, as I recall. So, as it was seasonal and to brighten and decorate the hall where the Social was held, the school was lent a load of beautiful decorations from a big store in Hamm called *Hortens*.

As I have said, our time at the school was strict, and we were only allowed into Hamm once a year for a couple of hours to do Christmas shopping before we went home. So, we often went to Hortens, a massive store like Harrods. I have looked it up, and it is no longer there, but it was huge in its day.

So, when they loaned the decorations, they were beautiful and expensive swathes of garlands and flowers to fill our hall.

When the Social was over, we were asked by the teachers if some of us could go and help clear the hall the next day and take down the decorations ready to go back to Hortens.

There was a rush of volunteers, mostly the younger girls, which my sisters were at that time. I think I was about fifteen, so I guess Lee and Debra, who are twins, were maybe twelve and a bit then.

I have talked to them recently about this incident. They both say they don't remember me doing the crime that they and others were involved with, and as I can't really remember, I have to take their word for what followed.

In short, the girls went to the hall to clear up after the party the night before. The teachers on duty had left dregs in glasses and half-empty bottles of the cheap wine *Deutsche Sekt* which the girls quaffed. Whole swathes of fancy garlands and trimmings were taken down. After bagging them up, the offending girls then took these from the hall and transported the bags up into the attic of our house where we lived. They then placed the trimmings in the empty cases and luggage, which were kept there waiting to be packed, ready for going home.

Thinking back, I don't know how they thought they would get away with it, but when the staff entered the hall later to find it stripped bare and no sign of the Christmas trimmings in the bags supplied from Hortens, there began a massive search and eventually, the trimmings were found. There was probably tinsel everywhere which was a clue.

I remember being called to see Miss Pointon, our Housemistress, to be told what had happened and that my sisters were among the girls involved. I'm sorry that whilst I was a little shocked, I found it quite funny.

Our matron, Frau Schroeder, who ruled the younger girls with a firm hand, went berserk, shouted, and told the girls off for their crime. My sisters remember her saying, 'I will schpit on you all,' as she was angry. Our mother was not pleased when she heard this. Of course, it was not a good reflection on us English girls being in their country too, and Windsor School did have a reputation to uphold.

The end result was that the girls were told that if they returned all the decorations to the bags in the Hall, Hortens would not call the police, so punishment was avoided.

We were due to go home for the Christmas holidays within a few days, so not a lot could be done in the way of punishment, but I think letters were written home to our parents. Our parents weren't happy about what had happened, but luckily no real harm had been done.

So, another brush with crime at Windsor ended – until I recount the times I escaped from school through the hole in the fence. But that is for another time.

Chapter Thirty-Six

A Memorable Performance

Just before the Christmas, now past, of 2021, I had a text from my old friend Ursula in Norwich, who told me some sad news. One of my firm favourites in music, Carlos from the group Il Divo, had just died. When I looked it up online, he had just gone on December 11th, 2021. The report said he was fifty-three, and apparently, he had a short illness and died of Covid complications. It was quite sudden, and like the other members of the group and his fans, I felt sad.

Il Divo was a group put together in 2003 by Simon Cowell, the big music mogul of, amongst other things, the X-Factor fame. He must have recognised their great talent and signed them to his record label.

The group consisted of four international opera and tenor singers, and Carlos was my favourite with his voice and cheeky smile. I had enjoyed their music from the beginning, and I bought their album *Ancora* in 2005. Hearing of his early demise inspired the *memorable performance* chapter where I write about seeing them perform at Blickling Hall just outside Norwich in July 2006.

Blickling Hall, a famous Jacobean Hall near Aylsham in Norfolk and the former home of Anne Boleyn (being of the Howard family) who is said to haunt it, is a big tourist attraction and a lovely place to visit.

For a few years, concerts and performances had been held on its extensive grounds with the house and lake as the backdrop. We had been to a couple of pop music shows held there before, but I was over the moon to see that Il Divo would be there along with the New Zealand opera star, Hayley Westenra, on the evening of July 22nd, 2006.

This quotation I have found from a report in the Norfolk daily paper, the Eastern Daily Press, about the anniversary of ten years of music performances at Blickling Hall. It describes perfectly what the atmosphere and ambience of such a show were like:

For several years at Blickling Hall, the same natural amphitheatre had swirled to the sounds of live summer music, but it was classical symphonies with a fireworks and laser light finale, played to a sedate audience dressed in black ties, posh frocks, sipping champagne and dining al fresco with picnic tables laden with fine food and candelabras.

Just as this extract describes, we arrived at the Hall's grounds in good time to get set up for our picnic and enjoy a wonderful evening. We did not have candelabra on the table, but a few people did, along with a huge trifle, I remember, with matching dishes in crystal glass bowls. Only the British can do it in style.

Many people were in the audience, and everyone was looking forward to the concert, even though the skies looked ominous with lots of black clouds above. I had bought our large over-the-head rain capes just in case and, as it turned out, just as well.

We saw Hayley Westenra – she was amazing, but when Il Divo appeared, everyone was enthralled by them and their singing.

I was in my element. I could see them on large screens on either side of the stage and in the flesh on the stage. In real life, they were much better than on TV. They performed for nearly an hour and were almost at the end of their set when the heavens opened. First, a few drops of rain and then more and more until it was a torrent. Much rushing around by us and others to don our rain capes and open umbrellas followed, but the show continued. Luckily the stage had a large overhead cover.

137

Our rain capes were good, but the rain went down the back of the loose neck of mine, and I was soaked to my knickers. I could cope, but Vic was not best pleased, and as soon as the fireworks were over, we grabbed our chairs and picnic pieces and made a dash for the exit and the car, along with many others.

Of course, by this time, the rain had stopped, being a typical short sharp English shower, but it was enough to soak you through. When I got to the car, I stood by the open door to remove my wet underwear, and needless to say, suddenly, a load of other people went by and saw everything. Typical, but by this time, I didn't really care.

We drove home on what then became a sunny evening. After an excellent performance and seeing Il Divo, we were glad to get back and change into some dry clothes. It was a memorable event all round.

Chapter Thirty-Seven

A Cultural Experience

In the early 2000s, I needed some changes in my life. It was the start of the new Millennium, and whether it was the change in me coupled with both my daughters living their own lives – one was married in 2001, and the other was at university, or whether it was just wanting something different, but I decided to leave my job at Norwich Union (now Aviva) and take a new path.

After the terrible attack on the Twin Towers in New York in 2001 (now known as 9/11), work had become stressful. The pensions I worked with were connected to the Stock Market, which meant people lost money daily. In addition, at work, we were bearing the brunt of our customers' frustrations, and after much thought, I decided to leave.

However, the loss of income would make a difference to our household, so I had to think of something. Then I remembered about NILE – This was the Norwich Institute for Language Education. An organisation set up in Norwich for furthering language skills of teachers of mainly English from other countries. I contacted them and discovered they were in dire need of homestay hosts to look after their students. We had two spare bedrooms, and after attending an open evening they held, we found out how it all worked. You had someone stay in your home as part of the family and looked after them and their needs and enjoyed the together time to help improve their English as well as learning a bit about them, their cultures, and the countries they were from. NILE paid you and expenses, so it was an all-round gain.

This began a new experience for us, and for about five years, we had many ladies come to stay with us. I opted for women teachers as that was my preference, and I knew we would have a lot to talk about and common interests, which proved to be the case.

Our first guest was a lovely lady from Italy called Marta. She stayed with us for a week, and we had an enjoyable time when she was with us. She was from Florence and said she was glad to be in England as it was much cooler than where she came from. The temperature often reaches over forty degrees in her home. After looking after her, she kindly rewarded us with cooking a lovely Italian spaghetti meal with lots of prawns. We were sorry to see her go but shortly after, we received our next guests from China, May and Jenny, who were English teachers in Guangzhou. This was when China had only recently opened their country and culture to overseas travel for its citizens. We later found out the Education departments at the various schools where the teachers worked paid for them to travel to the UK and come to Norwich for education improvements at NILE. We were the first introduction for the ladies who came to live with English families.

May and Jenny were married women with their own children, so we had similarities. Incidentally, they used English names as they told us we wouldn't have been able to pronounce their Chinese ones.

When I showed them around when they first arrived, they saw we had a tap on the outside back of our house. May wanted to know if that was where we washed the clothes, and when I told her *no,* she said was it in the bath upstairs? Again, I said *no* and told them I would do their washing in the machine, for which they were grateful. Also, when they unpacked, May had brought about fourteen toilet rolls with her in her case. I don't know what they thought English people did in that department. They also wanted to know if the bird table we kept in the back garden was to catch birds for us to eat.

They were lovely ladies, and we had them stay for a month because it was a long journey from China to the UK.

It was a success until they went to London for a weekend outing with NILE, and Jenny, the younger of the two staying with us, didn't come back with May. It transpired that she had arranged to meet her husband, who was in London presumably on business and consequently stay with him, and she went off. It was awful for May as well as the NILE people who had been responsible for them. Later, May had to pack up her case and things she had left with us to return to the NILE staff. I am sure Jenny would have been in a great deal of trouble with the authorities as their education department was strict.

Finally, before May left, she asked me if there were any shops in Norwich where she could get Clark's shoes. After I told her, she later came back with nine pairs of Clark's shoes for all the members of her family. Apparently, they were made in the city she came from, but they were too expensive for her to buy. A strange concept for us here.

It was a good experience on the whole, and we were happy to have more ladies visit from China. Then, at another time, we had Lily visit, and she stayed for three months and really did become part of the family. Vic even had her practising her English with a Norfolk accent.

She told us about life under Chairman Mao, who had been in power when she was a child, and we had many discussions about this. When we talked to her about the then one-child policy, which was in force, and she had a daughter, we asked her if it was true that some families sold their daughters as boys were preferable. She said, *Yes,* some had in the next village. It was difficult for us to come to terms with.

During the three months when Lily was with us, her group at NILE had many trips out at weekends, including to London, the Lake District and even Scotland. They were keen to see as much of the UK as possible. Lily knew all about Wordsworth and the Bronte sisters and loved English novels and literature. We had many interesting conversations together.

What I remember about the first trip they went on was being woken up at about six in the morning by the strong smell of cooking coming up the stairs from the kitchen. It turned out to be spare ribs, and the smell was potent. Lily and her colleagues had gone to the local Morrisons supermarket the day before. They bought loads of what we would call Chinese foods to take on their bus trip the next day. They didn't eat sandwiches for travelling like we did. What they took had to be cooked and heated up. The smells on the bus must have been quite strong.

Before she left us, Lily cooked us a lovely meal in the Chinese way, and we enjoyed it. We missed her when she left as she truly became a part of our family for a while, but we did keep in touch for a time.

After this, we had many visitors from France, Spain, Germany, Italy and Japan. Of course, not all at once, but the time spent together gave wonderful insight and understanding into how people lived in different countries.

Printed in Great Britain
by Amazon